THE *Sarcasm Handbook*

THE *Sarcasm Handbook*

The Only Book You'll Ever Need

Lawrence Dorfman
with James Michael Naccarato

Skyhorse Publishing

Skyhorse Publishing books may be purchased in bulk at special discounts for sales promotion, corporate gifts, fund-raising, or educational purposes. Special editions can also be created to specifications. For details, contact the Special Sales Department, Skyhorse Publishing, 307 West 36th Street, 11th Floor, New York, NY 10018 or info@skyhorsepublishing.com.

Skyhorse® and Skyhorse Publishing® are registered trademarks of Skyhorse Publishing, Inc.®, a Delaware corporation.

Visit our website at www.skyhorsepublishing.com.

10 9 8 7 6 5 4

Library of Congress Cataloging-in-Publication Data is available on file.

Cover design by Michael Short
Cover artwork: Shutterstock

ISBN: 978-1-5107-2326-9
eISBN: 978-1-5107-2327-6

Printed in China

Also by Lawrence Dorfman

The Snark Handbook
The Snark Handbook: Insult Edition
Snark the Herald Angels Sing
Snark Handbook: Sex Edition
Snark Handbook: Politics and Government
Snark Handbook: Clichés
Snark Handbook: Parenting
The Snark Bible
The Illustrated Dictionary of Snark
Schadenfreude
The Cigar Lover's Compendium

Author's Note

Hey, you. Yeah, that's right, you.

Trying to decide if this is worth laying out a few bucks at the cash register, or if you can get away with stuffing it in your pants and walking out? Is this really worth risking getting caught, arrested, and ending up sharing a 6' x 6' cell with Bubba? (That's *Mister* Bubba to you.)

So, here's the scoop of what you can expect.

There's a bunch of quotes.

I mean, it's not *Bartlett's Familiar Quotations*, but there's a good amount of people in here—famous, not-so-famous, infamous, and "who the hell is that" people who have shared their take on this off-kilter world we live in.

Then we have some jokes, one-liners, biting retorts.

Stuff to read instead of that must-read novel you wanted to crack open. (You know you're going to go through a bunch of reviews and then just *pretend* that you read it anyway. How many people do you think *actually* read Umberto Eco?)

It's easy. Perfect for those brief moments when you crave a smidge of entertainment and frivolity. Bite-sized. Just dip in, dip out. Yes, what you're holding is the perfect little book for the john. And don't forget to wash your hands.

Go now, no one's looking.

Clarification

You're going to see "*(S)" at points throughout this book.

This is the "emoticon" du jour to indicate the need for a sarcastic tone.

Let's give it a try:

Say "I'm trying to imagine you with a personality." *(S)

Again, aloud . . . this time with attitude.

(Sigh)

Alright, not bad. Not good either.

Stay with me and by the end of this book, you should have it mastered. [Optional *(S)—we'll just have to wait and see.]

Contents

THE *Sarcasm Handbook*

Introduction

"If you don't want a sarcastic answer,
don't ask me a stupid question."
—Unknown

In 2009, I lost my job in publishing.

The great geniuses *(S) who ran the company (and believe me there were many) decided that my position was no longer necessary—despite the fact that they didn't have a clue as to what I did or how I did it.

However, they did have the big desk, and after years of calling meetings and having lunches, they *knew* *(S) that without my position, there would be greater profit and bigger bonuses for all of them.

After all, they had been barely squeaking by on high six-figure salaries. *(S) And to be fair, publishing wasn't all that different from just about every other business at the tail end of the "I got mine" 90s, which had followed hot on the tail of the "Who can I screw now?" 80s.

On the street for the first time in my life, I jumped on the fun-filled carousel of job hunting, hoping to quickly grab that golden ring of job security and career fulfillment. After months of nausea and the vertigo of the interview process, I got a call from a friend who was an editor at a newish publisher and was looking to build a list.

She asked me if I wanted to write something.

I laughed. An author? Me?

I had spent a lifetime watching stay-at-home moms, overworked teachers, and road-weary salesmen approach the altar of fame and fortune with their blood-and-sweat-stained manuscripts only to be beaten back by self-righteous publishing folks critical of material that was too derivative, too original, too limited, too unfocused, too . . . unpublishable. "Thanks for playing, but don't let the door hit yr ass on the way out."

And they were the lucky ones.

Introduction

The poor slobs who were allowed to enter the arena typically found their heartfelt prose twisted, tweaked, sliced and diced. Their titles were discarded and their cover concepts designed by people who had never read a single word of their work. Demanding deadlines were enacted, penalties imposed, inflated print runs established.

And if by some very small chance it did well, you were committed to do it again . . . and again . . . and again . . . every year.

Did I want to add to the vast wasteland that book publishing had become? Was the next great American (or Lithuanian) novel percolating inside me, rife with product placement and "of the time" content that made it easier to tie in to advertising and sponsors?

Was I dying to explore some quasi-great figure from history or spew out a bio of some momentarily interesting musician or flash in the pan that *Rolling Stone* deemed hot?

Would my legacy be a commitment of time and energy in hopes of producing some great remainder-in-waiting, destined to sell at Barnes and Noble on the $4.98 table next to the *Pictorial History of the Merchant Marines?*

Oh, yes. Can I, can I please? *(S)

No, really. Can I, can I please?

I wanted to—no, *needed to*—prove to all those colleagues, through all those years, at all those publishing houses, that I could do it differently.

I would be an Author. (With a capital *A*.) Author!

But now I needed something to write about?

I was always a voracious reader. This was made easy by working in a business where free books were a major perk. Not much money for us lowly grunts in publishing, but all the books you can eat. *(S)

When I started, we got one free copy of every book that my company published. Every single one. Every bodice-ripping romance and no-taste diet cookbook. We had some mighty toasty fires those years. *(S)

Other sales reps were always sending me packages with new titles from their companies. Soon my name was added to a number of "big mouth" lists, where it was expected that I talk up the new book by Stephen King's wife's sister's nephew's babysitter's mother on the chance I could get someone to buy it. I would search through daily deliveries for the rare book that would be worthy of my "big mouth."

I sat comfortably in the wormhole of contemporary publishing and picked my target.

Introduction

One of the books I enjoyed reading recently was a thin tome called *Snark* by David Denby. Denby was a well-known critic for the *New Yorker*, a world-class snarkist, and sarcastic as all get out. But in this book, he took issue with the repartee that was prevalent at the time, making the point that snarky "shots" (mostly in political dissertation) were overtaking real thought and discussion. He saw snark and sarcasm as the lowest form of wit and humor and postured that it was ruining all conversation, creating a wasteland in personal relationships, and would possibly—no, probably—lead to the end of the world as we knew it. An interesting point I couldn't disagree with more.

I have always loved sarcasm and snark and have employed it almost from the moment I could speak. (Mama. DaDa. I'll smile when I'm good and ready. And who thought walking around with three pounds of cotton between my legs would help me learn how to walk? Sheesh.)

I was weaned on the television greatness of the Three Stooges and the Marx Brothers, and sat glued to the set watching the likes of David Steinberg, Jackie Mason, and Mort Sahl. When I got a little older, the joy of reading people like Kurt Vonnegut, John Barth,

Tom McGuane, Tom Robbins, and John Irving came into play. Later came David Sedaris, Carl Hiaasen, Jim Harrison, Christopher Moore, and many, many others. Cable brought me Sam Kinison, Bill Hicks, and Denis Leary.

So in 2009 I wrote *The Snark Handbook: A Reference Guide to Verbal Sparring.*

Got some nice reviews, lots of kudos from friends and colleagues . . . but barely a blip on the radar of the publishing movers and shakers who were off flying from the Frankfurt Book Fair to the London Book Fair to the Book Expo to . . . (Did they ever work?)

I decided I'd give them another chance with *The Snark Handbook: Insult Edition* in 2010.

Still busy.

I did *Snark the Herald Angels Sing* the next year.

Snark Handbook: Sex Edition the next.

Snark Handbook: Politics the next.

Snark Handbook: Parenting and *Schadenfreude* after that.

And the publishing world continued to ignore my brilliance. What was wrong with these people? How far did they have their heads up their . . .

I was done. Finished. Kaput.

Introduction

At least I got out before climbing into a bottle with F. Scott Fitzgerald or choking on an all-day sucker with Ernest Hemingway. *(S)

So when my publisher, a glutton for P&P (profit and punishment) *(S), called again and asked "Hey Snarky, wanna focus that red-hot wit of yours on SAR-CASM?" my first thought was: "Jeez, every time I think I'm out, they try to pull me back in."

Then, I thought "Cool, an advance."

And my third thought was "I'm hungry."

So, in reverse order, I ate a sandwich, planned how I would spend my advance, and called him back to say "Sure, why not?"

I'd give them another shot. I'm a ho.

Maybe they learned.

Maybe publishing had found its way back from the edge of the abyss of self-absorption and delusion to the ethical moral center of days of old.

Nah.

Well, there's always the $4.98 table at Barnes and Noble.

Definition of Sarcasm

"Some sarcasm is best told simply."
—KEVIN HART

sar·casm (sär͵kazəm) n. **1.** The use of irony to mock or convey contempt. **2.** Sharp, bitter or cutting expression or remark (may employ ambivalence). **3.** The use of words that mean the opposite of what you want to say, especially to show insult, show irritation, or be funny.

Ridicule, Scorn, Scoff, Sneer.
Yeah, *right.* *(**S**)

Defining sarcasm is like defining irony, or bullshit. It just can't be done. Try as hard as you like, all you can do is come reasonably close (and this ain't horseshoes). Defining sarcasm is elusive. It continues to slip just out of our reach. Words can never convey the pure essence of sarcasm; but like pornography, you'll know it when you see it.

Sarcasm: The Ability to insult idiots without them realizing it, or as Oscar Wilde once said, "The lowest form of wit but the highest form of intelligence."

Sarcasm vs. Snark

"Sarcasm is the body's natural defense
against stupidity."
—Anonymous

"So tell me Snarkboy, what's the difference between snark and sarcasm?"

Good question. Surprising, coming from you. What is the difference? As the unofficial arbiter of all things snark, (if you're not convinced, go back and read my six, yes count them, six previous books on snark. Go ahead, I'll wait . . . and my accountant will smile.)

Ready?

Okay, the answer, young grasshopper is . . . well, not much. Which is to say, it's subtle, very subtle. Sort of to-MAY-to, to-MA-to.

Sarcasm is usually filled with disdain. It's often mean, sometimes downright sadistic. "People say that laughter is the best medicine . . . your face must be curing the world!"

Snark is witty. It's clever repartee. It's showing off your smarts, without having anyone sighted in the scope of your aim. So then, why a book on sarcasm?

A *Scientific American* article written by Francesca Gino suggested that the use of *sarcasm* actually promotes creativity for those on *both* the giving and receiving end of sarcastic exchanges.

Imagine that.

I get to insult you, and you're smarter for it. (And yes, I didn't think that was possible.)

The key to mastering sarcasm is tone. And attitude. And wit. Oh, and, goes without saying, intelligence.

Maybe.

You can make the case that no one really needs a "handbook," that it's an innate thing that comes naturally to most humans (Americans in particular?) *(S) and it starts in the very young.

Sarcasm vs. Snark

Studies show that kids understand and use sarcasm as young as kindergarten. Some scientists say the inability to understand or recognize sarcasm is a telltale sign of brain disease.

Well, sure. But sarcasm can be easily misinterpreted, particularly when communicated via old-school mail or electronically. When you leave a voice message or, god forbid, are actually talking to another person, inflection, cadence, accent, emphasis, pitch, are essential communication tools. All of these nuances, coupled with facial expression and body language, can help make the target of your sarcasm (or the other persons you want to hear and get the joke) understand.

The world as we now know it is rife with sarcasm. This book maintains that, contrary to the pundits of yore, sarcasm can be—and is—an art. The problem, however, is that sarcasm easily gets lost in print.

Why?

I'll say it again. A crazy little thing called tone. Inflection.

Sayin' it again, Sparky: Tone is extremely important.

Indeed (wow that was pompous), many phrases can hold completely harmless and safe meanings until you apply tone.

The leader of the pack these days is, "Yeah, *right*." Try to go a day without hearing that one or uttering it yourself. It's a panacea to end all panaceas, a magic bullet that is used, when spoken correctly, to keep your enemies at bay, let your friends know how you feel, and to signal to the world, "Watch out, this one's skeptical."

But there are lots of others. For instance:

"With the greatest respect . . ."
"Thanks for the help . . ."
"Cool . . ."
"I'll make a note of that . . ."
"Take your time . . ."
"Obviously . . ."
"Sorry . . ." (With prerequisite eye roll)
"Great job . . ."
"Well done . . ."
"Oh, really?"
"Good luck with that . . ."
"I'm so happy for you . . ."
"Fascinating . . ."

One might feel that you're quite the nice fella or gal if you say any one of those tropes. "What a nice person!"

they might extol. But add even a modicum of sneer into the way you say those things . . . well, then you have sarcasm.

How and When to Use Sarcasm

"Blows are sarcasms turned stupid."
—GEORGE ELIOT

In the play *Oedipus the King*, by Sophocles, our hero must answer the following riddle: "What goes on four feet in the morning, two feet at noon, and three feet in the evening?"

Oedipus answers correctly with "man," and is then allowed to go onto Final Jeopardy. (I'd like to see how fast he would have solved the riddle of the Rubik's Cube?)

The use of sarcasm is a bit like Oedie's riddle: it changes as we age.

We all love it when kids say the darndest things. When asked "Where was the American Declaration of Independence signed?" one child wrote "at the bottom." (You can almost hear his full response—"where do you think it was signed, you idiot?") Answering the question, "Phil has one hundred candy bars. He eats ninety. What does Phil have now?" one kid wrote: "Diabetes. Who let him eat ninety candy bars?"

In the later eighties and early nineties, moviegoers flocked to the movies to see Bruce Willis provide the voice for Mikey in a series of *Look Who's Talking* movies. It was just adorable to hear smarmy Bruce's sarcastic voice coming from little Mikey. A year later they upped the ante with babies voiced by Roseanne Barr and Damon Wayans.

Sarcasm and kids—a winning combination.

We even accept it when those cutie-pies get a little older and turn into those sullen, antisocial adolescents we all love. It may piss us off a bit, but who's *really* surprised when your teenager rolls their eyes and answers the question "Why is everything on the floor?" with "gravity."

How and When to Use Sarcasm

And then, when we get older, and the hair we had on our head begins to reappear sticking out of our ears and noses, and life tinkers with our internal clocks, cruelly lengthening the distance from our bladder to the toilet, our sarcastic attitude makes us—go on, say it—*endearing*.

"Mom, you should get a hearing aid."

"How much do they cost?"

"They're usually about two thousand dollars."

"Okay, when you say something worth two thousand dollars, I'll get one."

What a dear.

But the true measure of how and when to use sarcasm falls into our early-to-mid adulthood, where it gets honed like a piece of Chicago Cutlery. Work, home, relationships, driving (oh, especially driving) is prime territory for your inner sarcasm to emerge like a phoenix from the ashes.

Has there been a time when you've heard "I'd like to see you in my office" and you haven't thought "and I'd like to see you under the tires of my car"? Don't you want to look that colleague in the eyes and say: "I can explain it to you, but I can't understand it for you"?

How many times have you been asked "can you take out the garbage" and bit your lip to keep from saying: "Okay, but you better grab your coat because it's cold out there"?

But the fertile crescent of sarcastic retorts is the swaddling, smothering world of relationships.

"I offended you with my opinion? You should hear the ones I keep to myself."

"I tried my best to see things from your point of view, but your point of view is stupid."

"If you have a problem with me, or with something I do, or did, or might do, just write it all down on a piece of paper . . . and then shove it up your ass."

Full Disclosure

There is a slight possibility that exercising your blossoming sarcastic abilities out loud may cause bodily harm, and/or having all your belongings piled up on your front lawn.

But once you get out of the ER, find a new place for all your shit, and have time to reflect, you'll see that it all was worth it.

Other Helpful *(S) Hints

Take notes from the people well-versed in it. The more time you spend around people who use sarcasm, the better you'll become.

And trust me, it ain't difficult to find people who use sarcasm these days.

Sarcastic Bastards in History

> "I was sorry to hear my name mentioned as one of the great authors, because they have a sad habit of dying off. Chaucer is dead, so is Milton, so is Shakespeare, and I am not feeling very well myself."
> —MARK TWAIN

These are the masters.

Learn from them, be inspired by them, and though you may never pass through the Asgardian gates and take your place among them, you will be better for having known them.

P. J. O'Rourke

(b. 1947) American journalist

"Always read stuff that will make you look good if you die in the middle of it."

"Giving money and power to government is like giving whiskey and car keys to teenage boys."

"When buying and selling are controlled by legislation, the first things to be bought and sold are legislators."

H. L. Mencken

(1880–1956) American journalist, cultural critic, and scholar of the English language

"Democracy is the theory that the common people know what they want, and deserve to get it good and hard."

"No one ever went broke underestimating the taste of the American public."

"Puritanism: The haunting fear that someone, somewhere, may be happy."

Sarcastic Bastards in History

Ambrose Bierce

(1842–1914?) American journalist, short story writer

"Love: A temporary insanity curable by marriage."

"Corporation, n. An ingenious device for obtaining individual profit without individual responsibility."

"Future. That period of time in which our affairs prosper, our friends are true and our happiness is assured."

Mark Twain

(1835–1910) American writer

"Whenever you find yourself on the side of the majority, it is time to pause and reflect."

"If you tell the truth, you don't have to remember anything."

"Don't go around saying the world owes you a living. The world owes you nothing. It was here first."

Jane Austen

(1775–1817) English novelist

"The person, be it gentleman or lady, who has not pleasure in a good novel, must be intolerably stupid."

"I do not want people to be very agreeable, as it saves me the trouble of liking them a great deal."

"A large income is the best recipe for happiness I ever heard of."

Jonathan Swift

(1667–1745) Irish writer

"When a true genius appears in this world, you may know him by this sign, that the dunces are all in confederacy against him."

"May you live all the days of your life."

"Vision is the art of seeing things invisible."

Sarcastic Bastards in History

George Saunders

(b. 1958) American writer

"We try, we fail, we posture, we aspire, we pontificate—and then we age, shrink, die, and vanish."

"Nostalgia is, 'Hey, remember the other mall that used to be there?'"

"So I may not have had a gothic childhood, but childhood makes its own gothicity."

Charles Portis

(b. 1933) American writer

"You must pay for everything in this world one way and another. There is nothing free except the Grace of God. You cannot earn that or deserve it."

"My Master of Arts degree means nothing at all to these monkeys and I have come to share their indifference."

"Lookin' back is a bad habit."

David Sedaris

(b. 1956) American writer

"I haven't got the slightest idea how to change people, but still I keep a long list of prospective candidates just in case I should ever figure it out."

"If you read someone else's diary, you get what you deserve."

"Writing gives you the illusion of control, and then you realize it's just an illusion, that people are going to bring their own stuff into it."

Christopher Moore

(b. 1957) American writer

"People, generally, suck."

"If you think anyone is sane you just don't know enough about them."

"Nobody's perfect. Well, there was this one guy, but we killed him."

Fran Lebowitz

(b. 1950) American writer

"In real life, I assure you, there is no such thing as algebra."

"Life is something that happens when you can't get to sleep."

"The opposite of talking isn't listening. The opposite of talking is waiting."

Great Moments in Sarcasm

Sarcasm, unlike politics, has had many great moments throughout history. It would be impossible to compile them all, so I include a few here for you to further your studies.

"Light travels faster than sound. This is why some people appear bright until they speak."
—Steven Wright

♦ ♦

"I'm sorry I hurt your feelings when I called you stupid. I thought you already knew."
—Unknown

"Mirrors can't talk. Lucky for you they can't laugh
either."
—UNKNOWN

♦ ♦

"He's the only man I ever knew who had rubber
pockets so he could steal soup."
—WILSON MIZNER

♦ ♦

"I'd tell you to go to hell, but I work there
and don't want to see your ugly mug every day."
—UNKNOWN

♦ ♦

"Some people stay longer in an hour than
others can in a week."
—WILLIAM DEAN HOWELLS

♦ ♦

"Many wealthy people are little more than janitors
of their possessions."
—FRANK LLOYD WRIGHT

♦ ♦

"People say that laughter is the best medicine . . . your
face must be curing the world!"
—UNKNOWN

Great Moments in Sarcasm

"He was happily married—but his wife wasn't."
—VICTOR BORGE

♦ ♦

"You go girl! And don't come back."
—UNKNOWN

♦ ♦

"I didn't attend the funeral, but I sent a nice letter
saying I approved of it."
—MARK TWAIN

♦ ♦

"I'm busy right now, can I ignore you some other time?"
—UNKNOWN

♦ ♦

"He has no enemies, but is intensely disliked by his
friends."
—OSCAR WILDE

♦ ♦

"I never forget a face, but in your case
I'll be glad to make an exception."
—GROUCHO MARX

♦ ♦

"Well, my imaginary friend thinks you
have serious mental problems."
—UNKNOWN

"If you've never met the devil on the road of life, it's because you're both heading in the same direction."
—UNKNOWN

♦ ♦

"A narcissist is someone better looking than you are."
—GORE VIDAL

♦ ♦

"Tell me . . . Is being stupid a profession
or are you just gifted?"
—UNKNOWN

♦ ♦

"I don't trust him. We're friends."
—BERTOL BRECHT

♦ ♦

"I'm not listening, but keep talking.
I enjoy the way your voice makes my ears bleed."
—UNKNOWN

♦ ♦

"I have never killed a man, but I have read many
obituaries with great pleasure."
—CLARENCE DARROW

Great Moments in Sarcasm

"I'm not your type. I'm not inflatable."
—UNKNOWN

♦ ♦

"Jealously is a disease . . . get well soon!"
—UNKNOWN

♦ ♦

"I need what only you can provide; your absence."
—ASHLEIGH BRILLIANT

♦ ♦

"If only closed minds came with closed mouths."
—UNKNOWN

♦ ♦

"Have you ever listened to someone and wondered,
'Who ties your shoes for you?'"
—UNKNOWN

♦ ♦

"Not all girls are made of sugar and spice and
everything nice. Some are made of sarcasm, wine, and
everything fine."
—UNKNOWN

"At a restaurant: 'Would you like a table?'
'No, I came here to eat on the floor.
Carpet for five, please?'"
—UNKNOWN

♦ ♦

"His mother should have thrown him away
and kept the stork."
—MAE WEST

♦ ♦

"Those who laugh last think slowest."
—UNKNOWN

♦ ♦

"I don't believe in plastic surgery but in your case . . ."
—UNKNOWN

♦ ♦

"Whoever said nothing was impossible obviously
never tried slamming a revolving door."
—UNKNOWN

♦ ♦

"Why don't you bore a hole in yourself and
let the sap run out?"
—GROUCHO MARX

Great Moments in Sarcasm

"If the grass is greener on the other side,
you can bet the water bill is a lot higher."
—UNKNOWN

♦ ♦

"The trouble with her is that she lacks the power of
conversation but not the power of speech."
—GEORGE BERNARD SHAW

♦ ♦

"If it looks like I give a damn, please tell me.
I don't want to give off the wrong impression."
—UNKNOWN

♦ ♦

"I'd agree with you but then we'd both be wrong."
—UNKNOWN

♦ ♦

"Silence is golden; duct tape is silver."
—UNKNOWN

♦ ♦

"Flying is learning how to throw yourself
at the ground and miss."
—DOUGLAS ADAMS

♦ ♦

"You sound better with your mouth closed."
—UNKNOWN

"I'm not sarcastic. I'm just intelligent
beyond your understanding."
—UNKNOWN

♦ ♦

"Children threaten to run away from home.
It's the only thing keeping parents going."
—UNKNOWN

♦ ♦

"If I knew I would live this long, I'd have taken
better care of myself."
—MICKEY MANTLE

♦ ♦

"I feel so miserable without you;
it's almost like having you here."
—STEPHEN BISHOP

♦ ♦

"That's the ugliest haircut I've ever seen yet
it compliments your face perfectly."
—UNKNOWN

♦ ♦

"We didn't lose the game; we just ran out of time."
—VINCE LOMBARDI

Movies

"Good evening, ladies and gentleman. My name is Orson Welles. I am an actor. I am a writer. I am a producer. I am a director. I am a magician. I appear onstage and on the radio. Why are there so many of me and so few of you?"
—ORSON WELLES

From the earliest days, the movies provided an escape from the tedium of everyday life. They made us laugh at the despair of Charlie Chaplin and the absurdness of the Marx Brothers, thrill to the adventures of Buck Rogers and Flash Gordon, and tap our feet to Busby Berkeley and Al Jolson. Then a funny thing happened.

The movies became relevant. They wanted to pull away the fabric of life and show us the dark, ugly underbelly. They became hyperreal, grotesque, and shocking. They were going to teach us something.

Can we honestly say we're better for it?

Today, we would arrest Gene Kelly for singing without a permit, Dorothy for zoning violations when she moved her house, and Fred Astaire for scuffing up the ceiling. Scarlet would be hauled off as an unfit mother, George Bailey would never climb out of the bottle at Nick's, and Dumbo would be rescued by PETA.

And we end up with innumerable opportunities to hone our sarcasm chops.

Movies

SPOILER ALERT: a collection of spoiled items that stinks up the place.

8 ½ (1963)
Director: Federico Fellini
Cast: Marcello Mastroianni, Claudia Cardinale, Anouk Aimée, Sandra Milo

Fellini's eighth-and-a-half film portrays a famous Italian film director struggling with "director's block." (As if there is such a thing.) He copes by having fantasies about the "perfect" woman while entertaining his mistress and his estranged wife. He meets with a Cardinal in a steam bath, dances with prostitutes, and ultimately finds happiness in the circus. Blake Edwards did it with Dudley Moore and a slo-mo Bo Derek and gave his a *10*.

ALL QUIET ON THE WESTERN FRONT (1930)
Director: Lewis Milestone
Cast: Lew Ayres, Louis Wolheim

Have you been to the western front? It's in a freakin' war. Quiet my ass.

AMERICAN BEAUTY (1999)

Director: Sam Mendes

Cast: Kevin Spacey, Annette Bening, Thora Birch, Wes Bentley, Mena Suvari, Chris Cooper, Allison Janney, Peter Gallagher

Depressed father, neurotic mother, homophobia, young girl infatuation, and a bullet to the head. It's all coming up roses.

AMERICAN PSYCHO (2000)

Director: Mary Harron

Cast: Christian Bale, Willem Dafoe, Jared Leto, Samantha Mathis, Chloë Sevigny, Reese Witherspoon

First of all, it's described as a black comedy/horror film. Huh? A rich investment banker enjoys using axes, nail guns, and chainsaws for his sadistic sexual enjoyment and our "amusement"? Of course, it became a Broadway musical.

. . . AND JUSTICE FOR ALL (1979)

Director: Norman Jewison

Cast: Al Pacino, Jack Warden, John Forsythe, Lee Strasberg, Jeffrey Tambor

A young man stopped for a routine traffic offense is mistaken for a killer who has the same name. He's sent to prison for something he didn't do, and he eventually kills himself. Meanwhile, a sadistic judge (played by John "Charlie's Angels" Forsythe) boasts about raping a young girl and expects the system to get him off. If this is justice, it's completely "out of order."

APOCALYPSE NOW (1979)
Director: Francis Ford Coppola
Cast: Marlon Brando, Robert Duvall, Martin Sheen, Frederic Forrest, Sam Bottoms, Larry Fishburne, Dennis Hopper

Vietnam. Enough said.

But just for the fun of it, let's say more. Martin Sheen had a heart attack during the filming. Marlon Brando showed up a gazillion pounds overweight (and earned $3.5 million for fifteen minutes of screen time). A typhoon destroyed most of the sets, causing months of delays. Instead of a projected three months to film, production took well over three years to finish, and went millions and millions and millions of dollars over budget. Good thing Charlie didn't surf—they wouldn't have been able to afford the surfboards.

ARSENIC AND OLD LACE (1944)
Director: Frank Capra
Cast: Cary Grant, Raymond Massey, Josephine Hull, Jean Adair, Jack Carson, Peter Lorre, Edward Everett Horton

Two lovely old sisters end the suffering of lonely old bachelors with a glass of elderberry wine spiked with arsenic, strychnine, and a just a hint of cyanide. Sounds like a new show on the Food Network.

AS GOOD AS IT GETS (1997)
Director: James L. Brooks
Cast: Jack Nicholson, Helen Hunt, Greg Kinnear, Cuba Gooding Jr.

Jack Nicholson is a racist, misanthropic, germophobic writer suffering from OCD who finds love with a single mother of a chronically ill boy. Yup. As good as it's going to get.

Movies

BACK TO THE FUTURE (1985)
Director: Robert Zemeckis
Cast: Michael J. Fox, Christopher Lloyd, Lea Thompson, Crispin Glover, AND Eric Stoltz (who originally was cast as the lead, but replaced after just weeks of filming)

Stoltz literally went back to the *past* (or at least the Dark Ages) when *Back to the Future* made more than $11 million at the box office opening weekend and turned Michael J. Fox into a megastar.

In the film, Marty McFly goes back in time where he accidentally becomes his mother's love interest and goes on to inspire Chuck Berry.

BATMAN MOVIES (1943–2018)
Directors: Tim Burton, Joel Schumacher, Christopher Nolan, Zack Snyder, and more
Cast: Michael Keaton, Val Kilmer, George Clooney, Christian Bale, Ben Affleck, among others

A millionaire playboy who has everything, acts out his angst by dressing as a bat to fight crime, allowing Jack Nicholson, Jim Carrey, and Heath Ledger to chew up all the scenery. But he gets to say in a hoarse, shouldn't-fool-anybody voice, "I'm Batman." Cool.

THE BIG LEBOWSKI (1998)
Director: Joel Coen
Cast: Jeff Bridges, John Goodman, Julianne Moore, Steve Buscemi, John Turturro

A group of misfit bowlers, led by not-the-*BIG* Lebowski, find themselves in the middle of kidnappings, ransoms, and the world of porn. I agree with them, "Fuck it. Let's go bowling."

BRIEF ENCOUNTER (1945)
Director: David Lean
Cast: Celia Johnson, Trevor Howard, Stanley Holloway

A suburban housewife has a chance meeting with a stranger at a train station. So far, so good. Then we watch for over an hour as she embarks on an affair, is accused of being a hooker, and contemplates suicide. She should have taken a cab.

CATCH-22 (1970)
Director: Mike Nichols
Cast: Alan Arkin, Bob Balaban, Martin Balsam, Richard Benjamin, Art Garfunkel (his acting debut), Jack Gilford, Charles Grodin, Bob Newhart, Anthony Perkins, Paula Prentiss, Martin Sheen, Jon Voight, and Orson Welles

Captain Yossarian wants to be mentally evaluated hoping he'll be found unfit to fly dangerous missions. He runs into a "Catch-22," which was actually created by the novel's author, Joseph Heller. It states that an airman would have to be *crazy* to want to fly more missions, and *sane* if he didn't want to. But if he was *sane*, then he would have to fly them. If he *flew* them, then he would be *crazy* and therefore he wouldn't have to; but if he didn't fly them, he was obviously *sane* and then he would have to fly them. Huh? That's some catch.

CHILDREN OF MEN (2006)
Director: Alfonso Cuarón
Cast: Clive Owen, Julianne Moore, Clare-Hope Ashitey, Michael Caine, Chiwetel Ejiofor, Charlie Hunnam

It's 2027, mankind is infertile, and civilization is about to collapse. Illegal immigrants flood the few countries with still functioning governments, but you need to have letters of transit to be allowed in. Outside of the whole infertility thing, sounds like things haven't changed much since *Casablanca* in 1942. Play it again, Sam.

A CLOCKWORK ORANGE (1971)
Director: Stanley Kubrick
Cast: Malcolm McDowell, Patrick Magee, Adrienne Corri, Miriam Karlin

Still more to look forward to in the near future. Ultra-violent gangs terrorize London. After gang leader Alex is caught, his rehabilitation is being forced to watch sex and violence with his eyes propped open, while listening to the music of Beethoven. In the sequel, he becomes the head of programming at Skinemax.

DAMN YANKEES (1958)
Director: George Abbott
Cast: Tab Hunter, Gwen Verdon, Ray Walston

The New York Yankees lose the play-offs after a Washington Senators fan makes a deal with the devil. Who knew the curse would last this long?

Movies

THE DAY THE EARTH STOOD STILL (1951)
Director: Robert Wise
Cast: Michael Rennie, Patricia Neal, Hugh Marlowe, Sam Jaffe

Aliens Klaatu and Gort stop by to visit Earth. They warn us that, if we do not join the universe in peace, Earth will be reduced to a "burned out cinder." Then they leave. Earth responds, "Fuck it. Let's go bowling."

DIE HARD (1988)
Director: John McTiernan
Cast: Bruce Willis, Alan Rickman, Alexander Godunov, Bonnie Bedelia

An off-duty NYC police officer visits his estranged wife in LA and stops a terrorist group from stealing $600 million in bearer bonds. "Vacation Hard," "Let's Meet for the Holidays Hard," and "How to Blow up an LA Skyscraper Hard" must have all been taken as titles. "Yippee-ki-yay, motherfucker."

DOG DAY AFTERNOON (1975)
Director: Sidney Lumet
Cast: Al Pacino, John Cazale, James Broderick, Charles Durning

Al Pacino is a first-time crook who tries to rob a Brooklyn bank to pay for his wife Leon's sex reassignment surgery. The thing is, there's no money in the bank. Hijinks ensue until Fredo dies.

DR. STRANGELOVE, OR: HOW I LEARNED TO STOP WORRYING AND LOVE THE BOMB (1964)
Director: Stanley Kubrick
Cast: Peter Sellers, George C. Scott, Sterling Hayden, Keenan Wynn, Slim Pickens

Jack D. Ripper, a depraved USAF General, orders a first strike nuclear attack on the Soviet Union. Former Nazi, Dr. Strangelove, helps to find a solution. And it's a comedy. "Gentlemen, you can't fight in here! This is the War Room."

Movies

DUCK SOUP (1933)
Director: Leo McCarey
Cast: Marx Brothers, Margaret Dumont

Mrs. Teasdale will provide much needed financial aid to the bankrupt country of Freedonia, if Rufus T. Firefly is appointed . . . forget it, who cares, it's the Marx Brothers. Why a duck? Because Lentil Soup would have given us gas.

FIDDLER ON THE ROOF (1971)
Director: Norman Jewison
Cast: Topol, Norma Crane, Leonard Frey, Molly Picon

A Jewish milkman deals with marrying off his daughters in a pre-revolutionary Russian village. On the other hand, there's something about tradition, Golde's dead grandmother, and a crazy fiddler perched on the roof trying not to break his neck. All this takes about three hours. Not a problem if I were a rich man, but jeez, some of us have to work.

FIGHT CLUB (1999)

Director: David Fincher
Cast: Brad Pitt, Edward Norton, Helena Bonham Carter, Meat Loaf, Jared Leto

Ed Norton plays a malcontent white-collar traveling automotive recall specialist. (The comedy potential for that is seemingly endless.) *(S) He meets up with a soap salesman (Pitt) and they create a club where men fight just for the fun of it. Just when you expect Clint Eastwood and an orangutan named Clyde to appear, it's revealed that Norton and Pitt are actually *the same person*! Say what? A clear example of writing a script "any which way you can."

FINIAN'S RAINBOW (1968)

Director: Francis Ford Coppola
Cast: Fred Astaire, Petula Clark, Tommy Steele

Years before Clemenza orders Rocco to leave the gun, and take the cannoli, Francis Ford Coppola embarked on a journey to take a 1947 stage musical and turn it into . . . I don't know, a dated, wildly-out-of-touch, forgettable 1968 movie musical. In fairness, the motion picture studios were gobbling up every Broadway show in sight—*West Side Story* (1961), *Gypsy* (1962), *The Music Man* (1962), *My Fair Lady* (1964), *Sound of Music* (1965), *Camelot* (1967), *Funny Girl* (1968), *Oliver!* (1968)—to name just a few.

And that's when God said (or maybe it was the movie going public): "Enough is enough!" Looking back and wondering why the hell he had agreed to make a musical starring a frail Fred Astaire and the one-hit wonder Petula "Downtown" Clark, I'm sure that's when he came up with the line "they made me an offer I couldn't refuse."

FISTFUL OF DOLLARS (1964)

Director: Sergio Leone

Cast: Clint Eastwood and a bunch of Italian actors with fake American names

The "Man with No Name" appears for the first time in this "Spaghetti Western," which reinvented the classic American western through an Italian production that was filmed in Spain and based on the Japanese film *Yojimbo*. Can't get much more authentic than that.

FRANKENSTEIN (1931)
Director: James Whale
Cast: Colin Clive, Mae Clarke, Boris Karloff

Let's get this straight right from the start. Boris Karloff did not play Frankenstein. He played Frankenstein's monster, or just the "monster." Colin Clive played Frankenstein, as in Dr. *Henry* Frankenstein. Gene Wilder played Dr. Frederick Frankenstein, pronounced "Fronkensteen," and Frau Blücher had great knockers. Got it?

GENTLEMEN PREFER BLONDES (1953)
Director: Howard Hawks
Cast: Marilyn Monroe, Jane Russell, Charles Coburn

An American showgirl searching for a husband and diamonds (not necessarily in that order) finds love, marriage, and an amazing pink dress by convincing an old coot that if she was his daughter he'd encourage her to prostitute herself for cash—as long as there was lots of it.

GONE WITH THE WIND (1939)
Director: Victor Fleming
Cast: Clark Gable, Vivien Leigh, Leslie Howard, Olivia de Havilland

So, this is what we know: Scarlett secretly loves Ashley, who will marry her cousin Melanie. Rhett overhears her declaration of unrequited love, and naturally falls in love with her on the spot. Then Scarlett marries Charles, who soon dies. Melanie is pregnant and Prissy "don't know nothin' about birthin' babies." Rhett marries Scarlett. They have a daughter. Rhett gets drunk and rapes Scarlett, then apologizes. Scarlett gets pregnant, then miscarries. Their daughter dies. Melanie dies. Superman dies. Rhett leaves Scarlett. She plans to think about it tomorrow. Oh yeah, and the Civil War is going on.

GOOD WILL HUNTING (1997)
Director: Gus Van Sant
Cast: Robin Williams, Matt Damon, Ben Affleck, Stellan Skarsgård, Minnie Driver

A self-taught South Boston genius works as a janitor at MIT where he anonymously solves difficult math problems left for genius grad students. He finds a smart girl, then loses smart girl. He finds a quirky therapist, but then turns down a dream job. He chucks it all and drives to California to find smart girl. Isn't this *Flashdance* with smart people?

GREASE (1978)
Director: Randall Kleiser
Cast: John Travolta, Olivia Newton-John, Stockard Channing, Eve Arden

A 1978 musical set in a 1958 High School. Thirty-year-old Olivia Newton-John starred as the virginal high school senior, and John Travolta played the goofy leader of the tough-as-Kleenex T-Birds, who somehow falls in love with the good girl. This all goes together like *rama lama lama ka dinga da dinga dong*. Or maybe more like *shoo-bop sha wadda wadda yippity boom de boom*.

GREAT ESCAPE (1963)
Director: John Sturges
Cast: Steve McQueen, James Garner, Charles Bronson, James Coburn, David McCallum, Richard Attenborough

A group of soldiers plan to escape from the escape-proof Stalag Luft III by smothering the camp with testosterone. Steve McQueen is so cool that not only is his escape cool, but he's cool when he's recaptured, and even more cool when he's placed in solitary confinement. I mean, *cool*.

HAIRSPRAY (2007)
Director: Adam Shankman
Cast: Nikki Blonsky, John Travolta, Michelle Pfeiffer, Christopher Walken

It's a shopping aisle dilemma. Which *Hairspray* to choose? Not the 1988 comedy film directed by John Waters, nor the 2002 Broadway musical. No, let's pick the 2007 musical film. Okay, so a plus-sized high school student finds love, achieves stardom, and integrates 1962 Baltimore all by appearing on the "Corny Collins Show." All in a day's work. Oh, and John Travolta plays her mom.

IT HAPPENED ONE NIGHT (1934)
Director: Frank Capra
Cast: Clark Gable, Claudette Colbert

A spoiled heiress runs away to rendezvous with her new husband but on the way she meets Clark Gable. Let's have a show of hands. Who thinks they'll be surprised by the ending?

IT'S A WONDERFUL LIFE (1946)
Director: Frank Capra
Cast: James Stewart, Donna Reed, Lionel Barrymore, Ward Bond

Truth in advertising disclaimer: For two hours, it is a real *sucky* life. George Bailey gets slapped by his boss, conned into taking over his father's business, and becomes disappointed by his newly married brother. Then, he blows his wedding money trying to keep his business afloat, is classified 4-F, is cheated by Old Man Potter, is punched in the face by Zuzu's teacher's husband, drives into a tree, and, not surprisingly, contemplates suicide. But then a bell rings, an angel gets his wings, and we all agree that George is the "richest man in town."

Movies

JAILHOUSE ROCK (1957)
Director: Richard Thorpe
Cast: Elvis and some other people

Elvis accidentally kills someone and ends up in the state penitentiary, where he discovers his musical ability. If he had only stayed there, we would have been spared *Tickle Me* (1965), where he played a singing rodeo rider; *Harum Scarum* (1965), where he's a singing would-be assassin; *Spinout* (1966)—singing race car driver; *It Happened At the World Fair*—singing crop duster; and *Paradise, Hawaiian Style* (1966)—singing helicopter pilot. If they had to let him out, couldn't they have locked up the screenwriters instead?

KING OF COMEDY (1982)
Director: Martin Scorcese
Cast: Robert De Niro, Jerry Lewis, Tony Randall, Sandra Bernhard

A mentally deranged stand-up comedian (which may be redundant) kidnaps Jerry Lewis and demands to be allowed to appear on his talk show. Of course, he's a hit and frankly nothing else matters.

LIFE OF BRIAN (1979)
Director: Terry Jones
Cast: Monty Python

Brian Cohen is a young Jewish boy who's born on the same day as AND next door to Jesus Christ. A madcap romp of mistaken identity continues right up to Brian's crucifixion. Accused by some as being blasphemous, others saw it as deeply religious and reverential. Nah. Just kidding. Pretty much everyone saw it as blasphemous and it was originally banned in several countries.

MUSIC MAN (1962)
Director: Morton DaCosta
Cast: Robert Preston, Shirley Jones, Buddy Hackett, Hermione Gingold

Harold Hill poses as a boys' bandleader to con naive Iowa townsfolk out of their hard-earned cash. After an elaborate scheme where he bilks the townsfolk out of their money for instruments, uniforms, and music instruction books, Hill gives them . . . instruments, uniforms, and music instruction books. He wins the hand of the virtuous librarian and the boys are transformed into a spectacular marching band. Now Harold is stuck in River City forever. You see, Harold Hill has entered that land of shadow and substance we like to call the twilight zone.

MY FAIR LADY (1964)
Director: George Cukor
Cast: Audrey Hepburn, Rex Harrison, Stanley Holloway, Wilfrid Hyde-White

A misogynistic and snobbish phonetics professor agrees to a wager that he can take a flower girl and make her presentable in high society. And who might that flower girl be? It's Audrey Hepburn. Really? Hey Professor Higgins, you want to win my money, what do you say we make Totie Fields presentable? Maybe Moms Mabley. I'd even settle for Roseanne. But Audrey Hepburn? Not happening.

ONE FLEW OVER THE CUCKOO'S NEST (1975)
Director: Milos Forman
Cast: Jack Nicholson, Louise Fletcher

Career criminal Randle McMurphy tries to beat the system by having his remaining prison sentence transferred to a mental institution. Unfortunately for him, the hospital is run by the anti-Christ Nurse Rat-shit, and she gets the last laugh. McMurphy gets a lobotomy. Hardly seems fair.

PAL JOEY (1957)
Director: George Sidney
Cast: Rita Hayworth, Frank Sinatra, Kim Novak

A womanizing singer falls for a naive chorus girl, but continues to romance a wealthy ex-girlfriend to get her to finance his nightclub. It all blows up (figuratively, not literally) and the singer and chorus girl walk off together, apparently to a Free French garrison at Brazzaville. Yes, Frankie, this could be the beginning of a beautiful friendship.

SAFETY LAST! (1923)
Directors: Fred C. Newmeyer and Sam Taylor
Cast: Harold Lloyd

Considered one of the great film comedies of all time, it starred Harold Lloyd (who?), cost $121,000 to make (how?), it's earned $1.5 million to date (what?), and it's almost one hundred years old (yawn!).

Movies

SILENCE OF THE LAMBS (1991)
Director: Jonathan Demme
Cast: Jodie Foster, Anthony Hopkins, Scott Glenn, Ted Levine

Brilliant, cannibalistic serial killer Hannibal Lecter leads FBI trainee Clarice Starling on a bizarre trip that involves decapitation, torture, and a suit made from real skin. Lucky for her he doesn't invite her for dinner.

SINGIN' IN THE RAIN (1952)
Director(s): Stanley Donen & Gene Kelly
Cast: Gene Kelly, Donald O'Connor, Debbie Reynolds, Jean Hagen

Sound comes to the movies, and Gene Kelly finds his new star Debbie Reynolds when he jumps into her cab to escape his adoring fans. That never happens to me. When I jump into a cab all I ever find is the stink of whatever food the driver ate for lunch three days ago. Times sure have changed.

THANK YOU FOR SMOKING (2005)
Director: Jason Reitman
Cast: Aaron Eckhart, Katie Holmes, Cameron Bright, Maria Bello, Joan Lunden

Big Tobacco spins the research on behalf of cigarettes, and a smarmy lobbyist has a bout with his conscience, but comes to his senses in time to defend the cell phone industry against claims they cause brain cancer. I felt like I needed a shower after seeing this.

TO KILL A MOCKINGBIRD (1962)
Director: Robert Mulligan
Cast: Gregory Peck, Mary Badham, Phillip Alford, Ruth White, and Robert Duvall as Boo

Got to tread lightly here. This is *gen-u-ine* first class American Literature. Widower lawyer Atticus Finch (Substitute Abraham Lincoln or Mahatma Gandhi, if you like) believes all people are to be treated fairly, even though the movie is set in Alabama in the early 1930s. Atticus is appointed to defend a black man who's accused of raping a white girl. You can guess things don't go too smoothly from this point.

When the real killer is finally unmasked and the kids are saved by Boo, the misunderstood recluse, they all agree it's better to make up an ending then reveal the truth. Then Boo arranges for Vito to meet the drug lord Sollozzo.

TREASURE OF SIERRA MADRE (1948)
Director: John Huston
Cast: Humphrey Bogart, Walter Huston, Tim Holt, Bruce Bennett, and little Bobby Blake.

Let's go to Mexico, team up with a couple of guys who we can't trust, follow a certifiably crazy prospector deep into the mountains to mine gold, and ignore the fact that there are always bandits ready to attack (but who apparently can't tell the difference between gold dust and sand). Oh, and when the bandits finally get what they deserve it's because a prepubescent Baretta ("Don't do the crime if you can't do the time") recognizes Bogart's donkey. Story continuity? We don't need no stinkin' story continuity.

THE USUAL SUSPECTS (1995)

Director: Bryan Singer
Cast: Kevin Spacey, Benicio del Toro, Stephen Baldwin, Gabriel Byrne, Kevin Pollak, Chazz Palminteri, Pete Postlethwaite

Verbal Kint weaves an increasingly complex confession about his involvement in a gang led by the mysterious Keyser Soze. Oh, and there's a coffee cup named after Pete Postlethwaite's character. The greatest trick the devil ever pulled was convincing the world they couldn't leave the theater to go to the bathroom during this film.

WAG THE DOG (1997)

Director: Barry Levinson
Cast: Dustin Hoffman, Robert De Niro, Anne Heche, Denis Leary, Willie Nelson

To distract the media from revealing a sex scandal that implicates the President of the United States just weeks before his re-election, a DC spin doctor creates a fake war with the help of a Hollywood producer. To keep it merrily spinning along, they create a war hero who was left behind enemy lines. When the real soldier whose name they had "borrowed" turns out to be criminally insane and is shot during an attempted rape, they turn it into a heroic death from wounds he sustained *during his rescue.*

I used to think this was a sarcastic black comedy. Now I know better. It's a documentary. Maybe it should be rereleased as *Wag the Dog, or How I Learned to Stop Worrying and Love Fake News.*

WHO'S AFRAID OF VIRGINIA WOOLF? (1966)
Director: Mike Nichols
Cast: Elizabeth Taylor, Richard Burton, George Segal, Sandy Dennis

Cute. The title is an obvious take-off on the tune "Who's Afraid of the Big Bad Wolf?" featured in Disney's *Three Little Pigs.* Clever. But then how the hell did it come to describe four foul mouth hyper-abusive drunks who, in the course of the film, deal with impotence, false pregnancy, abortion, infidelity, and an imaginary child. Damn. Virginia Woolf needs a better agent.

Sarcastic Quotes about Film

"I don't want to achieve immortality through my work. I want to achieve it through not dying."
—WOODY ALLEN

♦ ♦

"There are no rules in filmmaking. Only sins. And the cardinal sin is dullness."
—FRANK CAPRA

♦ ♦

"We don't make movies to make money; we make money to make more movies."
—WALT DISNEY

♦ ♦

"People have forgotten how to tell a story. Stories don't have a middle or an end anymore. They usually have a beginning that never stops beginning."
—STEVEN SPIELBERG

♦ ♦

"In England, I'm a horror movie director. In Germany, I'm a filmmaker. In the US, I'm a bum."
—JOHN CARPENTER

Movies

"Pain is temporary, film is forever!"
—JOHN MILIUS

◆ ◆

"Self-plagiarism is style."
—ALFRED HITCHCOCK

◆ ◆

"Nothing recedes like success."
—BRYAN FORBES

Music

"He has Van Gogh's ear for music."
—BILLY WILDER

Music can soothe the wild beast in us. Maybe. But growing up with head-banging, hip-gyrating, pelvis-grinding dancing, I wasn't so sure. And today, with all the elaborate tattooed, pierced, gender-neutral bodies, I'm betting there are quite a few wild beasts out there going: "I don't think so. Just give me a nice quiet spot on the savannah and some John Denver. You guys are all nuts." So, strap on your ear buds, suck at the teat of Spotify, and become one with the sacred nothingness of sarcasm in music.

Bands

A-HA—This 1985 one hit wonder's "Take On Me" was really nothing more than a soundtrack to an amazing music video. Just another classic from the way-back machine. But wait. The band has released *ten* studio albums and have plans for an acoustic tour in . . . 2018. Wow, that's the real a-ha moment. Guys, fire your publicity people because you couldn't be more invisible if you were Claude Rains. (Exactly, who even is that? Claude Rains played The Invisible Man in the classic Universal movie of the same name.)

ART OF NOISE—This would not be my first choice to name a musical act, especially if most of our tunes were instrumentals. I guess Bleeding Eardrums was taken.

BADFINGER—Doesn't this beg to have your fans show you their "bad" finger? What's it like to play to an audience who's always giving you the finger? And how do you know if they're fans or critics? Clue: if you're playing retirement homes, fans. Everywhere else, not so much.

Music

THE BAND—I know, let's go hear the Band tonight. Which band? The Band. What's the name of the band? The Band? Yes, what's the name of the band? That is the name, The Band. "That" is the name of the band? Why does it seem like I've heard all this before?

BLOOD, SWEAT & TEARS—Yeah, maybe in the beginning when Al Kooper was in the band and he brought a bit of the Blues Project chops with him, but by the time David Clayton-Thomas headlined they should have changed the name to Snap, Crackle, & Pop.

BLUE ÖYSTER CULT—Just pisses me off every time I have to figure out that stupid-ass umlaut. Don't fear the *typist*.

BUTTHOLE SURFERS—But of course . . . Honorable mention: Circle Jerks

CRASH TEST DUMMIES—Another name that is a result of a party-induced joke. If you spend that much time coming up with a name, I'll spend that much time giving you a listen.

DEAD KENNEDYS—Why? Because the band members didn't like the other possibility—Thalidomide. True Story.

DEVO—Yeah, we all know the name comes from their idea of de-evolution, blah, blah, blah. I like that one of the band's founders actually de-evolved all the way back to the most primitive plastic brick when he wrote the score for *The Lego Movie.* Is it just me DEVO, LEGO . . . DEVO, LEGO . . . Whip it good.

THE DOOBIE BROTHERS—All I got to say is truth in advertising.

THE FLAMING LIPS—Starts to make my Bleeding Eardrums sound better, doesn't it?

FOO FIGHTERS—An early name for UFOs. I once heard founder Dave Grohl explain that if he had known that this was going to last more than one album he probably would have come up with a different name. From Nirvana to the Foo Fighters, someone please teach Dave to take a little more time before making decisions.

Music

FRANKIE GOES TO HOLLYWOOD—This name was inspired by the movie career of Frank Sinatra. Too bad they didn't come close to his staying power. The band released two original albums and thirteen compilations. You know, come to think of it Sinatra recycled a lot of his movies, too.

THE FUGS—We all know what they wanted to be called. Just like every time those hard-ass detectives on *NYPD Blue* said "freakin'." Isn't it strange that a band can be called "Circle Jerks" but we can't call a band "Fuck" (either as a noun or a verb)?

THE GAP BAND—I am so disappointed. Apparently, the name comes from the streets in the band's original neighborhood—Greenwood, Archer, and Pine. Taylor Swift and I were thinking about an entirely different "gap."

GRATEFUL DEAD—This describes their fans to a "t." Could only have been better if they had called themselves "The Grateful Unwashed Dead."

GWAR—It's been said that the band's actual name is "God What an Awful Racket." Can't fault them for their honesty.

HOOTIE AND THE BLOWFISH—The band's name is based on nicknames lead singer Darius Rucker gave to two of his college friends. "Hootie," as Rucker referred to him, had an owl-like wide-eyed expression. His friend with puffy cheeks was nicknamed "Blowfish." I'm thinkin' that until Darius started making serious money, these two weren't his *best* friends.

HOOBASTANK—Where does this come from? The middle name of a former band member? No, that's not right. Ah, named for the German Hoobas Tank? Don't think so. Oh, it's a foreign word meaning "Hopscotch." Nah. It's a . . . you know what, I don't know and I don't give a shit. I'm never listening to them anyway.

HÜSKER DÜ—TWO UMLAUTS!!!

JEFFERSON AIRPLANE—What I find interesting is that just before the band crashed and burned, they changed the name to Jefferson Starship. Yup, sure fooled us.

LED ZEPPELIN—Supposedly Keith Moon suggested the name after hearing them. It wasn't flattering, more like "this will go over like a lead balloon." If he was looking for a better description, he might have come up with Self-Aggrandizing Egotists, but then we would have lost that great Hindenburg album cover.

MARILYN MANSON—I guess if I was Brian Warner of Canton, Ohio, and I wanted to be a rock star, I would want to change my name, too. Coming up with a combination of Marilyn Monroe and Charles Mansion, maybe not.

MEN AT WORK—Inspired by a road sign. Based on their one-hit career, "Wrong Way, Go Back" may have been more fitting. But maybe they do things differently "Down Under."

MR. MISTER—Sort of like the band The The, which leads us to the inevitable review, Suck Suck.

MOBY GRAPE—What's purple and swims in the ocean? Moby Grape. When I was a lad, nobody cared where the name came from. We just loved the fact that on their first album cover, drummer Don Stevenson is photographed giving the finger. How cool was that? It was cooler when the second pressing AIRBRUSHED it out, which meant someone had screwed it up the first time. How does something like that get by all those production people? Probably everyone was high and thinking "the next guy's gonna catch it."

MOLLY HATCHET—From the legend of Hatchet Molly, a prostitute that lured men to her home, then castrated and mutilated them. Sounds like a job for Marshall Tucker, who's used to rounding up Outlaws, probably with a .38 Special.

MÖTLEY CRÜE—This needs to stop. First of all, it's not pronounced as it should be with the umlauts. ("Metally Crooe-uh," anybody?) Nikki Sixx was once quoted as saying the use was "visual," suggesting a strong "German," "future belongs to us" vibe. This from a guy with a porn star name and magic marker stain on his chin? Sure it does.

MOTÖRHEAD—Really? Again? The late metal god Lemmy Kilmister admits to having borrowed it from Blue Öyster Cult. Why? Because it looked "mean." But this was from the guy who is quoted as saying "People don't become better when they're dead . . . People are still assholes, they're just dead assholes!" Mmmm.

MUDHONEY—From sexploitation auteur Russ Meyer's movie. Same is true for Faster Pussycat and Vixen. I guess there were no takers for Beneath the Valley of the Ultra-Vixens.

NICKELBACK—Originally called "The Village Idiots," Nickleback was born when band member Mike Kroeger worked at Starbucks and would often say "Here's your nickel back." Today they might have been called "Next in Line, Please!"

QUEEN—Talk about hiding in plain sight. The band is called "Queen" and the lead singer was, as described by one critic, a flamboyant, "posing, pouting, posturing tart" named Freddie Mercury. But when he finally comes out we're all surprised. What the hell were we thinking?

QUEENSRŸCHE—Queens-rue-y-cha. I'm sorry, that's the way it's pronounced. You play, you pay. Pretentious crap carries a price.

SEX PISTOLS—With Johnny Rotten and Sid Vicious, what can I say?

STEELY DAN—I love Steely Dan. That smooth jazz-rock-funk-R&B groove that gets your body just swayin' and movin' around your chair. (Yeah, I don't dance.) Just feelin' the music, reelin' from the harmonies. Hard to believe the name comes from a milk spurting strap-on dildo in William Burroughs's *Naked Lunch*. Go back, Jack, and do it again.

STONE TEMPLE PILOTS—So there's this STP Motor Oil (you see it all the time at NASCAR, Bubba) and they had a very popular logo. Singer-songwriter Scott Weiland and his band mates wanted to come up with a name that used those initials. Shirley Temple's Pussy lost out. Steven Tyler's Prostate would have been a viable option.

10CC—Story has it that 10cc is the amount of an average male's ejaculation. It's actually closer to 5. Based on the movies I watched in college, the band should have been called "Garden Hose of Semen."

THE VELVET UNDERGROUND—Avant-garde rock with Lou Reed and John Cale, managed by Andy Warhol, and named after a book on aberrant sexual behavior. Oh, and one of the most popular songs was "Heroin." How did these guys not have a Saturday morning cartoon show named after them?

THE WHO—This is difficult for me. I liked The WHO, but they're a hundred years old now. It's not a band name anymore; it's the response to "your grandkids are here to visit."

SOMEONE PLEASE TEACH MUSICIANS TO SPELL

a-Ha	Lynyrd Skynyrd
The Babys	Megadeth
The Black Crowes	The Monkees
Boyz II Men	Mudvayne
The Byrds	NOFX
Cyrkle	Outkast
Def Leppard	Phish
The Fixx	Ratt
Korn	Staind
Led Zeppelin	Stryper
Limp Bizkit	Siouxsie and the Banshees
Linkin Park	XTC
Ludacris	Yello

PLEASE KEEP MUSICIANS
AWAY FROM ATLASES

(Band names—and where they were formed)

ALABAMA—Fort Payne, Alabama

AMERICA –London, England

ASIA—London, England

BEIRUT—Santa Fe, New Mexico

BERLIN—Los Angeles, California

BLACK OAK ARKANSAS—Black Oak, Arkansas

BOSTON—Boston, Massachusetts

CHICAGO—Chicago, Illinois

EUROPE—Stockholm, Sweden

FLORIDA GEORGIA LINE—Nashville, Tennessee

JAPAN— London, England

KANSAS—Topeka, Kansas

THE MANHATTANS—Jersey City, Jersey

NAZARETH—Dunfermline, Scotland

ORLEANS—Woodstock, NY

PHOENIX—Versailles, France

Sarcasm in Music News

R.E.M. called it quits after thirty-one years together. Great, now I can get my religion back. Prepare for the inevitable "Greatest Hits" CD, following by the remastered box set, followed by the rarities box, followed by the tell-all book . . . Meanwhile, the B-52s have released the following statement: "We are now the coolest band out of Athens."

Eric Clapton, Paul McCartney, and Mick Jagger are all in their 70s. No word on a new Stones tour. Not until they hear from their new sponsors—Metamucil, Cialis, and Depends.

Tom Petty issued a "cease and desist" letter to Michele Bachmann's camp to prevent her from using "American Girl" for her campaign. She had been playing it to end her speeches. One lyric is, "God it's so painful when something that's so close is still so far out of reach." Not exactly confidence building, MB. Of course, I'm sure Willie Nelson would have let her use "Crazy."

Music

The Chinese government approved Bob Dylan's tour in that country. Evidently, it's the only country that can actually understand him.

More Bob. During the Grammys, a Los Angeles reporter on live TV started to speak in gibberish. Doctors chalked it up to a severe migraine ... although Bob Dylan said, "What's the big deal, I understood every word." At least we think that's what he said.

The Governor of Florida considered a pardon for Jim Morrison, some forty-one years after his infamous indecent exposure bust there. Talking about "Waiting for the Sun." Jeez, if Jim were alive today, he'd be spinning in his grave.

Still more Bob. It's been decided: a four-year-old boy has won a Bob Dylan sound-alike contest in Minnesota. He will accept the award as soon as he removes the clothespin from his nose.

U2 cancelled its tour, using Bono's bad back as an excuse. Doctors provided by Ticketmaster diagnosed it as a severe case of *Admittus Inflatus Valuitis*, or soft sales due to ridiculously overinflated ticket prices.

Again Bob, he's just too easy. A staff writer for the *New Yorker* resigned after admitting he faked quotes in a book he wrote about Bob Dylan. How the hell could anyone tell?

Stevie Wonder filed for divorce from his wife of eleven years and the mother of two of his children. Evidently, the couple couldn't see eye to eye on a number of issues.

British kid show host Jimmy Savile and washed up "rock star" Gary Glitter were indicted in a huge UK scandal involving hundreds of children over a number of years. Now, take a good look at their pictures. Are you telling me nobody saw that coming?

Mötley Crüe front man Vince Neil was arrested for driving his Lamborghini at high speeds while shit-faced in Vegas. The guy's forty-nine years old. Time to put the cork back in the bottle and call Dr. Drew, no?

Music

I get the whole rock-and-roll lifestyle thing, but every dog has his day . . . this isn't yours.

Icelandic singer Björk launched a campaign against a bid by Canada's Magma Energy, who is trying to buy up all of Iceland's energy sources. Word of advice, B? Don't wear the swan dress. SAPS ALL THE ENERGY RIGHT OUT OF THE ROOM.

Yoko held a press conference for a PBS show on John and the wacky meter went to eleven. Asked why she didn't leave NY after his death, she said to the reporter "you wouldn't go to a whorehouse if your wife died, would you" and claimed JL was the first man to push a baby stroller in public. She will be recording a remake of Paul Simon's "Still Crazy after All These Years."

Foxy Brown was arrested for continuing a feud with a neighbor that took out a restraining order against her. Foxy broke the order and allegedly "mooned her" in the process, although she denies it. "She says she saw my underwear, but I wasn't wearing any, so she's lying" . . . or maybe it's time to get the hedges trimmed back a little, Fox.

Sarcastic Quotes about Music

"I'm sick to death of people saying we've made eleven albums that sound exactly the same. In fact, we've made twelve albums that sound exactly the same."
—ANGUS YOUNG (AC/DC)

◆ ◆

"Music is the wine that fills the cup of silence."
—ROBERT FRIPP

◆ ◆

"All the good music has already been written by people with wigs and stuff."
—FRANK ZAPPA

◆ ◆

"I can't listen to that much Wagner.
I start getting the urge to conquer Poland."
—WOODY ALLEN

◆ ◆

"I don't know anything about music.
In my line you don't have to."
—ELVIS PRESLEY

Music

"Music is everybody's possession. It's only publishers who think that people own it."
—JOHN LENNON

◆ ◆

"I understand the inventor of the bagpipes was inspired when he saw a man carrying an indignant, asthmatic pig under his arm. Unfortunately, the manmade sound never equaled the purity of the sound achieved by the pig."
—ALFRED HITCHCOCK

◆ ◆

"I've been imitated so well I've heard people copy my mistakes."
—JIMI HENDRIX

◆ ◆

"After I saw Jimi [Hendrix] play, I just went home and wondered what the fuck I was going to do with my life."
—JEFF BECK

◆ ◆

"I love to sing, and I love to drink scotch. Most people would rather hear me drink scotch."
—GEORGE BURNS

"Talking about music is like dancing about architecture."
—STEVE MARTIN

◆ ◆

"I don't deserve a Songwriters Hall of Fame Award. But fifteen years ago, I had a brain operation and I didn't deserve that, either. So I'll keep it!"
—QUINCY JONES

◆ ◆

"I never had much interest in the piano until I realized that every time I played, a girl would appear on the piano bench to my left and another to my right."
—DUKE ELLINGTON

◆ ◆

"I don't like country music, but I don't mean to denigrate those who do. And for the people who like country music, denigrate means 'put down.'"
—BOB NEWHART

◆ ◆

"Let me be clear about this: I don't have a drug problem, I have a police problem."
—KEITH RICHARDS

Music

"We believed that anything that was worth doing was
worth overdoing."
—STEVEN TYLER

♦ ♦

"When I was a little boy, I told my dad,
'When I grow up, I want to be a musician.'
My dad said: 'You can't do both, Son.'"
—CHET ATKINS

Television and Entertainment

"I find television very educating. Every time somebody turns on the set, I go into the other room and read a book."
—GROUCHO MARX

Television is God's way of telling us too much of a good thing sucks. In the early days of TV we had three channels. Actually, two and a half. (ABC was so fuzzy we could only see about half of the program.) But we loved it. Company would come over just to see television programs. Saturday night boxing. *Bonanza* in color. *The Ed Sullivan Show,* where you could see bears riding bicycles, followed by the Rolling Stones, and then a man talking to his hand that had lips painted on it. And you couldn't wait for next week.

Today, we have five gazillion channels. Sitcoms aren't funny, dramas are predictable, and the news is fake. But I can watch it all on my phone! Too bad the content quality didn't keep up with the technology.

Sarcasm in Television and Entertainment News

"It's like getting an old dog back from the rescue pound. It's grateful to see you, and the relationship is still intact." That was the way Simon Cowell described being reunited with Paula Abdul. Ah yes, ever the charmer—the Michael Vick of the Entertainment industry.

It was announced that HBO had planned to follow up their biopic of Phil Spector with one on Fatty Arbuckle, starring Eric Stonestreet from *Modern Family*. One question . . . will Coke be a sponsor? (Obscure, but find Kenneth Anger's *Hollywood Babylon* if you want to read more.)

The Bravo channel scheduled *Real Housewives of New Jersey* on Sundays, following *Mob Wives*. Bravo was borrowing a page from NBC's advertising book by creating a new campaign along the lines of "Must-See TV." "Sundays on Bravo—Must have a full-frontal lobotomy to enjoy TV"

The show runner for *Cougar Town* spent a lot time looking for new names for the show to woo viewers that were put off by its original title. I've watched this Courtney Cox vehicle once or twice—how about "Friends, With Benefits"?

Yes, I know *Jersey Shore* has been off the air for some time but it's so easy . . . when they went to Italy, several cast members bought copies of a Rosetta Stone course, I guess using the time to finally learn some English.

MTV's *Jersey Shore* house is available for rent. For a mere $2,500, you can shower where the Sitch cleansed himself or sleep in the same bed as Snooki did. I personally would make sure that the entire gang from CSI Miami, NY, and Vegas get in there and luminol the entire place first. Just sayin'.

Crystal Harris, Hugh Hefner's ex-fiancée, told Howard Stern they only had sex once and that it was over "in two seconds." Not sure if she can count that high but hell, Hef, you're eighty-five and she's twenty-four. I am impressed with the two.

Television and Entertainment

New York City named an upper Manhattan street after the late, great George Carlin. George Carlin Way is in Morningside Heights near his old neighborhood. I'm sure he'd feel honored. I'm also sure that he would have preferred the street be called "ShitPissFuckCuntCocksuckerMotherfuckerTits Avenue." The only problem would have been getting companies to open new stores there.

Brigitte Nielsen claimed that in 1985, while Arnold Schwarzenegger was dating Maria Shriver, she and the future ex-Governor had an affair. Seems that Arnold shared his broadsword while the two of them were filming *Red Sonja*. Ms. Nielsen's dating history also included Sly Stallone and Flavor Flav. Guess she's really turned on by men who have difficulty stringing two cohesive sentences together.

Disney trademarked the name "Seal Team 6." Guess the geniuses there think the operation was carried out by actual seals (it's Disney, after all).

Nicholas Cage was arrested in New Orleans, drunk and arguing loudly with his wife. When the police arrived, they told them to "just go home." He responded, "Why don't you arrest me?" The cops again said "go home" and he repeated his taunt. So, they did and charged him with domestic abuse and disturbing the peace—only because it's still not an actual crime to be a total asshole.

Larry King, who says his first love is comedy, organized a one-man comedy revue called *Larry King: Stand Up.* "A man walked into a bar, and boy, did it hurt!"; "Hear about the broken pencil? It had no point!"; "Hey, I was reading a book about adhesive the other day. I just couldn't put it down."; "Why were my suspenders arrested? For holding up my pants." He knows these jokes from vaudeville—where he first saw them performed live.

George Clooney, when asked in an interview about his presidential aspirations, said "I've fucked too many chicks and did too many drugs to run," to which Bill Clinton replied, "Well son, it all depends on what you think is 'too many.'"

Television and Entertainment

It's true, Mike Tyson contributed to O Magazine's poetry issue. I understand he's got an ear for it. Actually, he's got a number of ears for it. Hopefully, he didn't bite off more than he could chew.

Megan Fox told an interviewer that she thought co-star Olivia Wilde is just "so sexy it makes me want to strangle a mountain ox." ??? Well, I do love me a good euphemism.

Randy Quaid and his wife sought asylum in Canada, claiming they feared a group they described as "Hollywood star whackers." Wouldn't that be a great name for a reality show? A combination of TMZ and the Whack-A-Mole game from the arcade—I might actually watch that one.

A TV host in New Zealand was forced to resign after he mocked the name of an Indian official, Sheila Dikshit. Weird, I tried for ten minutes and couldn't think of anything funny to say about the name Sheila.

The preserved body of Trigger, Roy Rogers's horse, was sold at an auction by Christie's for more than

$250,000. Also up: Roy's dog Bullet, Trigger Jr., and Buttermilk, all stuffed and mounted . . . no word on Dale Evans.

Dennis Rodman has written a children's book called *Dennis the Wild Bull*. Bookstores will shelve it in the alternative lifestyles section, next to *Heather has Two Mommie*s and *Hello, Sailor*, as the main character spends much of the book in a dress and has a stormy relationship with Ferdinand.

Glenn Beck claims he was treated rudely by the crew on an American Airlines flight because of his political views. Come on, Glenn. You were treated rudely by the crew of an American Airlines crew because you were a passenger on an American Airlines flight. And because you're Glenn Beck.

James Bond's iconic silver Aston Martin DB5, the one used in *Goldfinger* and *Thunderball*, has sold for over four million dollars at auction. *Plus* tax. A car collector from Cincinnati bought the car. Ah, the lengths some guys will go to get laid.

Sarcastic Quotes about Television and Entertainment

"I didn't like the play, but then I saw it under adverse conditions—the curtain was up."
—GROUCHO MARX

◆ ◆

"So long as there's a jingle in your head, television isn't free."
—JASON LOVE

◆ ◆

"Television is a medium because anything well done is rare."
—FRED ALLEN

◆ ◆

"How many times have you been watching an episode of *South Park* and thought, 'I'd like to be able to watch this on my television while hooked into my mobile device, which is being controlled by my tablet device which is hooked into my oven, all while sitting in the refrigerator'?"
—TREY PARKER

◆ ◆

"I turned up the brightness control on my TV but it didn't work. The show got even dumber."
—GREG TAMBLYN

"In Beverly Hills . . . they don't throw their garbage away. They make it into television shows."
—WOODY ALLEN

♦ ♦

"Watching cable news because you want to be informed is like going to Olive Garden because you want to live in Italy."
—ANDY BOROWITZ

♦ ♦

"Television is chewing gum for the eyes."
—FRANK LLOYD WRIGHT

♦ ♦

"If it weren't for Philo T. Farnsworth, inventor of television, we'd still be eating frozen radio dinners."
—JOHNNY CARSON

♦ ♦

"Life doesn't imitate art, it imitates bad television."
—WOODY ALLEN

$\mathcal{L}$iterature

> "Reading made Don Quixote a gentleman.
> Believing what he read made him mad."
> —GEORGE BERNARD SHAW

It is said that the earliest example of sarcasm in literature can be found in the Bible. In the Book of Genesis, God asks Cain if he knows where his brother Abel is. Clearly a test for Cain, who replies: "I don't know. Am I my brother's keeper?"

It is also the first example of *cojones* in the Bible. Cain had already killed his brother and was what? Looking to get away with it? There's like four people in Eden. Did he really think God didn't know? Maybe he had been away on business? Clearly our ancient common ancestor wasn't the sharpest knife in the drawer.

Later in the Book of Exodus, the Israelites ask Moses: "Was there a lack of graves in Egypt, that you took us to die in the wilderness?" Now remember, they had been slaves in Egypt. It was there that Pharaoh had ordered all newborn boys thrown into the Nile. And it was there that God had sent ten rockin' plagues to force the Pharaoh to release them. So, it was pretty ballsy to get in Moses's face.

Shakespeare's "Lend me your ears" speech in *Julius Caesar* is filled with sarcasm as Mark Antony repeatedly calls the murderer Brutus "noble" and "honorable." I also can't stop hearing Mark Antony scream "Stella" at the bottom of the stairs, but maybe that's just me. Literature is the devil's elixir for sarcasm, and Lucifer is high as a kite. Let's drink to that!

Literature

Sarcasm in Literary News

The Edgar Allan Poe House and Museum in Baltimore, where Ed lived for four years, frequently struggles with financing and actually closed for a year because of cuts in the budget. Got me to thinking. Maybe city officials should try to sell it. It would make a great starter house for some family—except for that constant thumping under the floorboards and all those damn ravens.

Marvel Comics's "new" *Spider-Man* is half-black and half-Latino and hails from Brooklyn. Hell, make him a Hasidic Jew and you have the comic book equivalent of *Do the Right Thing*.

The Board of Education (or is it "bored") in Kingston, NY, forced the high school production of *And Then There Were None* to revise all posters, signs, and programs. Why you ask? Because they contained an incendiary racist image—a noose. Now I get it, the noose is a powerful image, and unfortunately it was used in too many heinous race-based crimes. But this play is based on Agatha Christie's best-selling novel, AND there's a noose used in the play. It's far from racist. It'd be like banning the movie *Halloween* because there a scene with someone wearing a sheet, or lumping having a cross on your lawn with having a *burning* cross on your lawn.

Sarcastic Quotes about Literature and Writing

"He has never been known to use a word that might send a reader to the dictionary."
—WILLIAM FAULKNER
(ABOUT ERNEST HEMINGWAY)

♦ ♦

"Poor Faulkner. Does he really think big emotions come from big words?"
—ERNEST HEMINGWAY
(ABOUT WILLIAM FAULKNER)

♦ ♦

"The only thing I was fit for was to be a writer, and this notion rested solely on my suspicion that I would never be fit for real work, and that writing didn't require any."
—RUSSELL BAKER

♦ ♦

"I hate editors, for they make me abandon a lot of perfectly good English words."
—MARK TWAIN

"I love deadlines. I like the whooshing sound they
make as they fly by."
—DOUGLAS ADAMS

◆ ◆

"My Personality is 85 percent the last book I read."
—UNKNOWN

◆ ◆

"It took me fifteen years to discover I had no talent for
writing, but I couldn't give it up because by that time I
was too famous."
—ROBERT BENCHLEY

◆ ◆

"When ideas fail, words come in very handy."
—GOETHE

◆ ◆

"He was such a bad writer, they revoked
his poetic license."
—MILTON BERLE

◆ ◆

"Sarcasm is lost in print."
—JON CRYER

◆ ◆

"Literature is all, or mostly, about sex."
—ANTHONY BURGESS

Literature

"To write is human, to edit is divine."
—STEPHEN KING

♦ ♦

"If you write one story, it may be bad; if you write a
hundred, you have the odds in your favor."
—EDGAR RICE BURROUGHS

♦ ♦

"How often we recall, with regret, that Napoleon once
shot at a magazine editor and missed him and killed
a publisher. But we remember with charity, that his
intentions were good."
—MARK TWAIN

♦ ♦

"Finishing a book is just like you took a child out in
the backyard and shot it."
—TRUMAN CAPOTE

♦ ♦

"There is nothing to writing. All you do is sit down at
a typewriter and bleed."
–ERNEST HEMINGWAY

♦ ♦

"Most of the basic material a writer works with is
acquired before the age of fifteen."
—WILLA CATHER

"Nothing stinks like a pile of unpublished writing."
—SYLVIA PLATH

♦ ♦

"Coleridge was a drug addict. Poe was an alcoholic. Marlowe was killed by a man whom he was treacherously trying to stab. Pope took money to keep a woman's name out of a satire then wrote a piece so that she could still be recognized anyhow. Chatterton killed himself. Byron was accused of incest. Do you still want to a writer—and if so, why?"
—BENNETT CERF

♦ ♦

"I took a speed-reading course and read *War and Peace* in twenty minutes. It involves Russia."
—WOODY ALLEN

♦ ♦

"It is perfectly okay to write garbage—as long as you edit brilliantly."
—C. J. CHERRYH

♦ ♦

"When Shakespeare was writing, he wasn't writing for stuff to lie on the page; it was supposed to get up and move around."
—KEN KESEY

Literature

"Most writers can write books faster than publishers can write checks."
—RICHARD CURTIS

✦ ✦

"Tomorrow may be hell, but today was a good writing day, and on the good writing days nothing else matters."
—NEIL GAIMAN

✦ ✦

"Never throw up on an editor."
—ELLEN DATLOW

✦ ✦

"We write frankly and fearlessly but then we 'modify' before we print."
—MARK TWAIN

✦ ✦

"I love being a writer. What I can't stand is the paperwork."
—PETER DE VRIES

✦ ✦

"Never lend books, for no one ever returns them; the only books I have in my library are books that other folks have lent me."
—ANATOLE FRANCE

"If you start with a bang, you won't end with a whimper."
—T. S. ELIOT

♦ ♦

"Writing is turning one's worst moments into money."
—J. P. DONLEAVY

♦ ♦

"Books had instant replay long before televised sports."
—BERT WILLIAMS

♦ ♦

"Nothing, not love, not greed, not passion or hatred, is stronger than a writer's need to change another writer's copy."
—ARTHUR EVANS

♦ ♦

"This must be a gift book. That is to say a book, which you wouldn't take on any other terms."
—DOROTHY PARKER

♦ ♦

"Draw your chair up close to the edge of the precipice and I'll tell you a story."
—F. SCOTT FITZGERALD

Literature

"Outside of a dog, a book is man's best friend. Inside of a dog it's too dark to read."
—GROUCHO MARX

◆ ◆

"I am irritated by my own writing. I am like a violinist whose ear is true, but whose fingers refuse to reproduce precisely the sound he hears within."
—GUSTAVE FLAUBERT

◆ ◆

"My wife joined a book club.
They primarily read wine labels."
—UNKNOWN

◆ ◆

"Don't be dismayed by the opinions of editors, or critics. They are only the traffic cops of the arts."
—GENE FOWLER

◆ ◆

"I thought to myself, why not write a bestseller. In the first place, more people read them, you make more money, and it doesn't take any more time to write a bestseller than it does to write a book that nobody buys."
—GEORGE BURNS, FROM
THE THIRD TIME AROUND

"Writing is not necessarily something to be ashamed of,
but do it in private and wash your hands afterwards."
—ROBERT A. HEINLEIN

◆ ◆

"A library is a place where you can lose your innocence
without losing your virginity."
—GERMAINE GREER

◆ ◆

"Easy writing makes hard reading."
—ERNEST HEMINGWAY

◆ ◆

"A good novel tells us the truth about its hero; but a
bad novel tells us the truth about its author."
—GILBERT K. CHESTERTON

◆ ◆

"A writer never has a vacation. For a writer, life
consists of either writing or thinking about writing."
—EUGENE IONESCO

◆ ◆

"I heard that Amazon has started a program to try to
get people to trade in their old bound books to get an
electronic reader. They call it 'Kindling.'"
—KATE DEIMLING

Literature

"Half my life is an act of revision."
—John Irving

◆ ◆

"Make him [the reader] think the evil,
make him think it for himself, and you are
released from weak specifications."
—Henry James

◆ ◆

"Never judge a book by its movie."
—J. W. Eagan

◆ ◆

"The most valuable of all talents is that of never
using two words when one will do."
—Thomas Jefferson

◆ ◆

"Confidence is going after Moby Dick in a rowboat
and taking the tartar sauce with you."
—Zig Ziglar

◆ ◆

"A young musician plays scales in his room
and only bores his family. A beginning writer,
on the other hand, sometimes has the misfortune
of getting into print."
—Marguerite Yourcenar

"You can't judge a book by its cover but you can sure
sell a bunch of books if you have a good one."
—JAYCE O'NEAL

♦ ♦

"I get up in the morning, torture a typewriter
until it screams, then stop."
—CLARENCE BUDINGTON KELLAND

♦ ♦

"The book trade invented literary prizes
to stimulate sales, not to reward merit."
—MICHAEL MOORCOCK

♦ ♦

"A poet can survive everything but a misprint."
—OSCAR WILDE

♦ ♦

"We publish only to satisfy our craving for fame;
there's no other motive except the even baser
one of making money."
—THOMAS BERNHARD

♦ ♦

"Great is the art of beginning,
but greater is the art of ending."
—HENRY WADSWORTH LONGFELLOW

Literature

"It's called publishing. It's how smart people install
new ideas into other people's brains."
—STEVEN MAGEE

♦ ♦

"I hate writing, I love having written."
—DOROTHY PARKER

♦ ♦

"I suspect that one of the reasons
we create fiction is to make sex exciting."
—GORE VIDAL

♦ ♦

"One of the hardest things for a writer
to do is delete words."
—ALESSANDRA TORRE

♦ ♦

"All the words I use in my stories can be found
in the dictionary—it's just a matter of arranging
them into the right sentences."
—SOMERSET MAUGHAM

♦ ♦

"There is no great writing, only great rewriting."
—JUSTICE LOUIS BRANDEIS

"Inside every fat book is a thin book trying to get out."
—UNKNOWN

◆ ◆

"Authors who moan with praise for their editors always
seem to reek slightly of the Stockholm syndrome."
—CHRISTOPHER HITCHENS

◆ ◆

"I have written—often several times—
every word I have ever published."
—VLADIMIR NABOKOV

◆ ◆

"Writing without revising is the literary equivalent of
waltzing gaily out of the house in your underwear."
—PATRICIA FULLER

◆ ◆

"Fiction writing is great.
You can make up almost anything."
—IVANA TRUMP, UPON FINISHING HER FIRST NOVEL

◆ ◆

"Making love to me is amazing. Wait, I meant:
making love, to me, is amazing. The absence of two
little commas nearly transformed me into a sex god."
—DARK JAR TIN ZOO

Literature

"All writers are vain, selfish and lazy, and at the very bottom of their motives lies a mystery. Writing a book is a long, exhausting struggle, like a long bout of some painful illness. One would never undertake such a thing if one were not driven by some demon whom one can neither resist nor understand."
—GEORGE ORWELL

♦ ♦

"A professional writer is an amateur who didn't quit."
—RICHARD BACH

♦ ♦

"The road to ignorance is paved with good editors."
—GEORGE BERNARD SHAW

♦ ♦

"Kill your darlings, kill your darlings, even when it breaks your egocentric little scribbler's heart, kill your darlings."
—STEPHEN KING

♦ ♦

"Everything that is written merely to please the author is worthless."
—BLAISE PASCAL

Politics

"Reader, suppose you were an idiot. And suppose you were a member of Congress. But I repeat myself."
—MARK TWAIN

As we enter the hallowed halls of politics, I suspect you're wondering: "What can I possibly learn about sarcasm here?" We'll be rubbing shoulders with the most honorable and dedicated men and women this great country has to offer; men and women who unselfishly sacrifice their lives and devote all their energy to improving and protecting the lives of the public they represent; men and women who allow their lives and the lives of their families to be open books, free of all suspicion and suggestions of impropriety. We have gone too far to tarnish these great patriots by suggesting there is anything we can learn from them about sarcasm.

Maybe, but that's *not* my shoulder they're rubbing.

Sarcasm in Political News

The Washington Post reported that federal agencies will start saving the American public tons of money by purchasing things in bulk. Right. And my luck, that's the guy I get behind the next time I'm at Costco.

Among the many things alleged by Joe McGuiness in his book about Sarah Palin is that she had a one-night stand with NBA star Glen Rice, who was a junior playing for Michigan when she was a TV sports reporter. Sarah's response? "Hey, does that make me a Kardashian?" (Sorry, no for you.) Keith Olbermann trumps Palin for the emoticon, "Figures that the only pass Glen Rice ever made was at Sarah Palin."

Michelle Bachmann, the once and, God forbid, future candidate, showed off her "keen sense of humor" when she said she would never use a teleprompter if she was in the White House. "I would do it the old-fashioned way. I would write it on my hand." *Cue Scarecrow song*

Newt Gingrich once said in an interview that the adoption of same-sex marriage in New York showed the nation is "drifting toward a terrible muddle" and that the nation should be defending the federal Defense of Marriage Act, which defines marriage as being between a man and a series of women.

Our favorite topic Sarah Palin caused a minor scandal when her bus tour stopped at Mount Vernon, home of her favorite founding father. The problem occurred when someone from the press asked "Are you going to Mount Vernon?" and she replied "Who's Vernon?"

Sarah Palin (I told you) said in an interview when asked about whether she'd ever run for President, "I have a fire in my belly." Sarah, please, I'm beggin' ya, take a coupla Tums and lay down. It'll pass. You'll feel better. We'll all feel better.

Newt Gingrich says his passion for our country contributed to his marital infidelity. Huh? "So, my fellow Americans, if elected president as an uber-patriotic American, I'll be screwing just about everybody, all in the name of passionate patriotism." I can see him singing it now: "My country 'tis of thee, I love adultery, it makes me hard."

A married NY congressman was forced to resign after being caught answering a hook-up ad on Craigslist. The numbskull used his own name and posted a half-naked pic. But the worst part? The entire text was peppered with "LOL" maybe the acronym stands for "Lie on Lie." Just astounding.

The State Department asked Iran to release two hikers who were captured and taken hostage—by tweet. A spokesperson sent President Ahmadinejad a "birthday" message via Twitter and then urged him to consider releasing the two Americans. I don't know, but if it was me I think I could say "the full force and power and fury of the United States military will be all over your ass" in 140 characters or less? They should've just asked @realDonaldTrump.

Several congressmen said that Stephen Colbert's testimony on immigration was "inappropriate" and "an embarrassment." Well, if anybody knows the meaning of "inappropriate" and "embarassment," it would definitely be a member of Congress.

A federal judge ruled that the State of Massachusetts is responsible for paying for a sex-change operation for a prison inmate to become female from male. The con might want to change his mind again once he finds out he'll only get paid 80 percent of his weekly prison wages as a female.

This week's tally of Paul Ryan accomplishments: invented the Internet; created Cirque Du Soleil; was the second man to walk on moon; stole Pamela Anderson from Tommy Lee (something about "anatomy"); wrote the Bible; AND conceived the original idea for *50 Shades of Grey*. If only he could get Congress to represent the American people, he'd have a pretty good week.

A number of students at Harvard were investigated for allegedly cheating in a class called "Introduction to Congress." Yeah, you can't make this stuff up. Some were kicked out of school, but all is not totally bleak:

Politics

The students with the best fake grades get internships at *The Hill*.

Broad smiles are not allowed on New Jersey driver's licenses. You must stare into the camera stoically. Officials claim it's a matter of security. Might be a good idea. After six hours of waiting in the various lines at the DMV, anyone smiling that broadly would have to be a serious security risk.

Ah, yes—the Fourth of July. Independence Day. Picnics, drinking, and fireworks. And yet, one in four Americans does not know who we declared our independence from. One in four. And they all vote. I'm surprised that Dog the Bounty Hunter isn't our current president.

A Pakistani protester died after inhaling fumes from an American flag he was burning. Karma's a bitch, no? Only thing better would be seventy-two virgins waiting for him in the afterlife . . . and they all look like Betsy Ross.

City officials of Santa Cruz and an independent coffee shop fought over the shop's right to employ topless baristas. There was coverage on the local newscast, but they interviewed a patron who had been there all day. He talked so fast no one could understand him. Twenty-two cappuccinos will do that. "Vente, please . . ."

The Colorado Department of Higher Education suspended Greenway University in Denver, the country's only state-certified medical marijuana training school. Once informed, the response from the instructors was, "Huh?"

Officials in Baghdad wanted the United States to pay one billion dollars for the damages done to the city. I've seen before and after pictures . . . we owe 'em about a $1.80.

A Utah lawmaker lobbied to make the Browning .45 the state firearm . . . ? I get birds, flowers, trees, mottos, songs . . . but firearms? What's next? State booze? State drug of choice? Why stop? Go totally insipid: State bagel . . . State iPhone app . . . Hey, wait a minute, that's not a bad idea.

Politics

A former mayor of Fort Wayne, Indiana, who served for four terms and was one of the city's most popular leaders, won't get a new government center named for him because of the jokes his moniker could inspire. Harry Baals (pronounced just the way you think) is the current favorite in online voting, but two members of the city council, Anita Head and Holden McGroin, have refused to allow it.

Sarcastic Quotes about Politics

"Politics, it seems to me, for years, or all too long,
has been concerned with right or left instead
of right or wrong."
—RICHARD ARMOUR

♦ ♦

"The only difference between the Democrats
and the Republicans is that the Democrats allow
the poor to be corrupt, too."
—OSCAR LEVANT

♦ ♦

"Our 'neoconservatives' are neither new nor
conservative, but old as Babylon and evil as Hell."
—EDWARD ABBEY

♦ ♦

"A politician needs the ability to foretell what is going
to happen tomorrow, next week, next month, and next
year. And to have the ability afterwards to explain
why it didn't happen."
—WINSTON CHURCHILL

♦ ♦

"In the land of the blind, the one-eyed man is king."
—ERASMUS

Politics

"Politicians and diapers should be changed
frequently and all for the same reason."
—José Maria de Eça de Queiroz, translated
from Portuguese

♦ ♦

"Anarchism is democracy taken seriously."
—Edward Abbey

♦ ♦

"Since a politician never believes what he says,
he is quite surprised to be taken at his word."
—Charles De Gaulle

♦ ♦

"Hell, I never vote for anybody, I always vote against."
—W. C. Fields

♦ ♦

"When buying and selling are controlled by
legislation, the first things to be bought and
sold are legislators."
—P. J. O'Rourke

♦ ♦

"We live in a world in which politics
has replaced philosophy."
—Martin L. Gross, from
A Call for Revolution

"The death of one is a tragedy, but death of a million is just a statistic."
—MARILYN MANSON

♦ ♦

"Mothers all want their sons to grow up to be president but they don't want them to become politicians in the process."
—JOHN F. KENNEDY

♦ ♦

"There are many men of principle in both parties in America, but there is no party of principle."
—ALEXIS DE TOCQUEVILLE

♦ ♦

"I do know that the slickest way to lie is to tell the right amount of truth—then shut up."
—ROBERT A. HEINLEIN,
FROM *STRANGER IN A STRANGE LAND*

♦ ♦

"Those who are too smart to engage in politics are punished by being governed by those who are dumber."
—PLATO

Politics

"All of us who are concerned for peace and triumph
of reason and justice must be keenly aware how small
an influence reason and honest good will exert upon
events in the political field."
—ALBERT EINSTEIN

◆ ◆

"A good politician is quite as unthinkable
as an honest burglar."
—H. L. MENCKEN

◆ ◆

"Statesmen tell you what is true even though it may
be unpopular. Politicians will tell you what is popular,
even though it may be untrue."
—ANONYMOUS

◆ ◆

"I never did give them hell. I just told the truth, and
they thought it was hell."
—HARRY TRUMAN

◆ ◆

"Take our politicians: they're a bunch of yo-yos.
The presidency is now a cross between a popularity
contest and a high school debate, with an encyclopedia
of clichés the first prize."
—SAUL BELLOW

"A politician thinks of the next election—a statesman
of the next generation."
—JAMES FREEMAN CLARKE

♦ ♦

"In order to become the master,
the politician poses as the servant."
—CHARLES DE GAULLE

♦ ♦

"Corrupt politicians make the other
ten percent look bad."
—HENRY KISSINGER

♦ ♦

"Now I know what a statesman is;
he's a dead politician. We need more statesmen."
—BOB EDWARDS

♦ ♦

"Politicians are the same all over. They promise to
build a bridge even where there is no river."
—NIKITA KHRUSHCHEV

♦ ♦

"Status quo, you know, is Latin for 'the mess we're in.'"
—RONALD REAGAN

Politics

"Politics is the art of looking for trouble, finding it whether it exists or not, diagnosing it incorrectly, and applying the wrong remedy."
—ERNEST BENN

◆ ◆

"Liberalism is trust of the people tempered by prudence. Conservatism is distrust of the people tempered by fear."
—WILLIAM E. GLADSTONE

◆ ◆

"In my many years I have come to a conclusion that one useless man is a shame, two is a law firm, and three or more is a congress."
—PETER STONE

◆ ◆

"When I was a boy I was told that anybody could become President; I'm beginning to believe it."
—CLARENCE DARROW

◆ ◆

"Practical politics consists in ignoring facts."
—HENRY ADAMS

◆ ◆

"Truth is not determined by majority vote."
—DOUG GWYN

"The Supreme Court has ruled that they cannot
have a nativity scene in Washington, DC.
This wasn't for any religious reasons.
They couldn't find three wise men and a virgin."
—JAY LENO

◆ ◆

"Nowhere are prejudices more mistaken for truth,
passion for reason and invective for documentation
than in politics."
—JOHN MASON BROWN

◆ ◆

"Democrats think the glass is half full. Republicans
think the glass is theirs."
—UNKNOWN

◆ ◆

"Have you ever wondered why Republicans are so
interested in encouraging people to volunteer in their
communities? It's because volunteers work for no pay.
Republicans have been trying to get people to work
for no pay for a long time."
—GEORGE CARLIN

Politics

"Politics is the gentle art of getting votes from the poor and campaign funds from the rich, by promising to protect each from the other."
—OSCAR AMERINGER

♦ ♦

"Politics is the art of looking for trouble, finding it whether it exists or not, diagnosing it incorrectly, and applying the wrong remedy."
—ERNEST BENN

♦ ♦

"Every two years the American politics industry fills the airwaves with the most virulent, scurrilous, wall-to-wall character assassination of nearly every political practitioner in the country—and then declares itself puzzled that America has lost trust in its politicians."
—CHARLES KRAUTHAMMER

♦ ♦

"A promising young man should go into politics so that he can go on promising for the rest of his life."
—ROBERT BYRNE

"The Constitution is not an instrument for the government to restrain the people, it is an instrument for the people to restrain the government—lest it come to dominate our lives and interests."
—PATRICK HENRY

♦ ♦

"When they call the roll in the Senate, the Senators do not know whether to answer 'Present' or 'Not Guilty.'"
—THEODORE ROOSEVELT

♦ ♦

"The Democrats are the party that says government will make you smarter, taller, richer, and remove the crabgrass on your lawn. The Republicans are the party that says government doesn't work and then they get elected and prove it."
—P. J. O'ROURKE

♦ ♦

"How do you tell a Communist? Well, it's someone who reads Marx and Lenin. And how do you tell an anti-Communist? It's someone who understands Marx and Lenin."
—RONALD REAGAN

Politics

"We believe that to err is human.
To blame it on someone else is politics."
—HUBERT H. HUMPHREY

◆ ◆

"We have, I fear, confused power with greatness."
—STEWART UDALL

◆ ◆

"We have the best government that money can buy."
—MARK TWAIN

◆ ◆

"I have a problem with people who take the
Constitution loosely and the Bible literally."
—BILL MAHER

◆ ◆

"For the powerful, crimes are those that others commit."
—NOAM CHOMSKY, FROM *IMPERIAL AMBITIONS:
CONVERSATIONS ON THE POST-9/11 WORLD*

◆ ◆

"A lot has been said about politics; some of it
complimentary, but most of it accurate."
—ERIC IDLE

◆ ◆

"Don't vote, it only encourages them."
—BILLY CONNOLLY,
FROM *AN AUDIENCE WITH BILLY CONNOLLY*

"I have left orders to be awakened at any time during national emergency, even if I'm in a cabinet meeting."
—RONALD REAGAN

♦ ♦

"If I wanted to go crazy I would do it in Washington because it would not be noticed."
—IRWIN S. COBB

♦ ♦

"Politicians are people who, when they see light at the end of the tunnel, go out and buy some more tunnel."
—JOHN QUINTON

♦ ♦

"In this country American means white. Everybody else has to hyphenate."
—TONI MORRISON

♦ ♦

"I love to go to Washington—if only to be near my money."
—BOB HOPE

♦ ♦

"A conservative is one who admires radicals centuries after they're dead."
—LEO ROSTEN

Politics

"He knows nothing; and he thinks he knows everything. That points clearly to a political career."
—GEORGE BERNARD SHAW, FROM *MAJOR BARBARA*

♦ ♦

"After two years in Washington, I often long for the realism and sincerity of Hollywood."
—FRED THOMPSON

♦ ♦

"Half of the American people have never read a newspaper. Half never voted for President. One hopes it is the same half."
—GORE VIDAL, FROM *SCREENING HISTORY*

♦ ♦

"I remember when I first came to Washington. For the first six months you wonder how the hell you ever got here. For the next six months you wonder how the hell the rest of them ever got here."
—HARRY S. TRUMAN

♦ ♦

"An appeaser is one who feeds a crocodile, hoping it will eat him last."
—WINSTON S. CHURCHILL

"Just because you do not take an interest in politics
doesn't mean politics won't take an interest in you."
—PERICLES

♦ ♦

"The mystery of government is not how Washington
works but how to make it stop."
—P. J. O'ROURKE

♦ ♦

"I offer my opponents a bargain: if they will stop telling
lies about us, I will stop telling the truth about them."
—ADLAI STEVENSON, CAMPAIGN SPEECH, 1952

♦ ♦

"You have to remember one thing about the
will of the people: it wasn't that long ago that
we were swept away by the Macarena."
—JON STEWART

♦ ♦

"Instead of giving a politician the keys to the city,
it might be better to change the locks."
—DOUG LARSON

♦ ♦

"Absolute power does not corrupt absolutely, absolute
power attracts the corruptible."
—FRANK HERBERT

"The reason there are so few female politicians is that
it is too much trouble to put makeup on two faces."
—Maureen Murphy

◆ ◆

"Anyone who is capable of getting themselves made
President should on no account be allowed to do the job."
—Douglas Adams,
from *The Restaurant at the End
of the Universe*

◆ ◆

"Members of Congress should be compelled to wear
uniforms like NASCAR drivers, so we could identify
their corporate sponsors."
—Caroline Baum

◆ ◆

"You show me a capitalist, and I'll show you a bloodsucker."
—Malcolm X

◆ ◆

"If God wanted us to vote,
he would have given us candidates."
—Jay Leno

◆ ◆

"A nation of sheep will beget a government of wolves."
—Edward R. Murrow

"All people are born alike—
except Republicans and Democrats."
—GROUCHO MARX

♦ ♦

"The oppressed are allowed once every few years
to decide which particular representatives of the
oppressing class are to represent and repress them."
—KARL MARX

♦ ♦

"The politicians were talking themselves red,
white and blue in the face."
—CLARE BOOTHE LUCE

♦ ♦

"Too bad that all the people who know how to run the
country are busy driving taxicabs and cutting hair."
—GEORGE BURNS

♦ ♦

"Politics is supposed to be the second-oldest
profession. I have come to realize that it bears a very
close resemblance to the first."
—RONALD REAGAN

Politics

"I'm completely in favor of the separation of Church and State. . . . These two institutions screw us up enough on their own, so both of them together is certain death."
—GEORGE CARLIN

♦ ♦

"A politician is a fellow who will lay down
your life for his country."
—TEXAS GUINAN

♦ ♦

"In politics, stupidity is not a handicap."
—NAPOLÉON BONAPARTE

♦ ♦

"Politics, n: [Poly 'many' + tics 'blood-sucking parasites']"
—LARRY HARDIMAN

♦ ♦

"I predict future happiness for Americans, if they can prevent the government from wasting the labors of the people under the pretense of taking care of them."
—THOMAS JEFFERSON

♦ ♦

"There ought to be one day—just one—when there is open season on senators."
—WILL ROGERS

"Illegal aliens have always been a problem in the
United States. Ask any Indian."
—ROBERT ORBEN

♦ ♦

"We hang the petty thieves and appoint the great ones
to public office."
—AESOP

News

> "The more wonderful the means of communication,
> the more trivial, tawdry, or depressing its contents
> seemed to be."
> —ARTHUR C. CLARKE

Hey, here's an idea . . . READ! LEARN! LISTEN!

Without a doubt, knowing what's going on in the world will be your biggest friend in your quest to use sarcasm to its best advantage. Any idiot can be sarcastic, but in order to take it to the level of a Jedi, you have to know what you're talking about.

Sarcasm in the News

A Connecticut man was placed on probation after successfully using the negative side effects of an erectile dysfunction medication as his defense for the lewd acts he committed in public that initially led to his arrest. The probation will keep him from having to do hard time, but he will have to pay a stiff fine.

A Florida man in a wheelchair with no place to sleep was attacked by a twenty-year-old female "vampire." Taking refuge on the porch of a closed Hooters, the elderly man told the girl to come out of the rain and he would wait with her for her ride. He fell asleep but woke when she pounced on him and said she was a vampire. He got away and called the cops, who found her half-naked and covered in blood. Yikes. For real? Or the next Stephanie Meyer novel?

A woman with a large Afro had her hair searched for bombs at an Atlanta airport. In related news, a suicide bomber, with explosives hidden in his hair under his turban, killed a former Afghan president. Better safe than sorry as these new "coiffure bombs" evidently all have a hair trigger.

A kindergartener in Missouri brought a bag of crystal meth and a crack pipe to school for show and tell. It got out of hand when, before the teacher could stop it, the boy had the entire class re-enacting the party scenes from *Breaking Bad*.

Brazilian federal police arrested an Irish man with nearly two pounds of cocaine in his gut after X-Rays showed he had swallowed seventy-two packets. He was taken to a hospital, where he expelled the capsules. Now imagine tossing ten pints of Guinness on top of that and you have the winner of the First Annual Colin Farrell award.

FBI tapes show that Martin Luther King was a big fan of hiring hookers for sex parties whenever he came to Washington. Some critics who have said that his most famous sermon was plagiarized are pointing to this as proof: When told by the Madam he used in DC that he was a good customer, there would be no charge, he responded, "Free at last, free at last . . ." (Ouch, that's going to get some letters.)

The first Big Balls Award (hereafter know as a BBA) goes to the 290-pound Neanderthal from New York, who sued the White Castle chain for violating his civil rights by not making their booths bigger to accommodate his girth. Believe me, there's not a booth in America to accommodate an ass that big.

The Alaskan asswipe mother of the year who made her child drink hot sauce as punishment and then went on Dr. Phil was originally going to jail for a year, with a ten-thousand-dollar fine and ten years probation. Not gonna happen. She got three years probation. I think her son said it best: "uck you, ommy, you psycho itch."

Russian engineers are planning to launch a hotel that will orbit the Earth in space. If you thought room service was slow before . . .

A truck accident near Nashville involved the spilling of a number of canisters of bull semen headed to Texas for breeding. Authorities closed the highway until a

News

sufficient amount of Kleenex, towels, and gym socks could be brought in to facilitate a proper clean-up.

"Greek Police Smash Violent Doughnut Ring." That was the headline from Fox News. Had to read it twice. What exactly *is* a violent doughnut? Do you wait until it gets old and hard then toss it with extreme force? Upon further investigation, I learned that the police had to go undercover to break up a gang of strong-arm goons who were trying to monopolize the doughnut market in Thessaloniki, Greece. Which made me think, "Cops and doughnuts? Exactly how many months were these guys undercover?"

A thirteen-year-old Scottish girl was diagnosed with a rare disease in which brushing her hair could kill her. Evidently, the static electricity generated could shut down her brain. I suspect this is far more prevalent than we first suspected—Russell Brand, Zach Galifianakis, Jack Black, and Joaquin Phoenix all come rushing to mind.

A British woman, when charged with a hate crime for beating up a lesbian in a bar, bared her posterior to the court to show off a gay rights tattoo. Sort of an "Ass, Don't Tell" defense. The bobbies got her out of there quickly in kind of a bum-rush.

An Alabama company called Holy Smoke is offering to pack the ashes of cremated loved ones into various ammunitions so that mourners can take them along on "one last hunt." The ammo comes in shotgun size, handgun size, whatever you want. My fat Uncle Phil filled a howitzer shell.

A computer presided over a wedding in Texas. Using a monitor with a "virtual" minister on one side and the text on the other, the couple was married by the PC after an ordained friend was unable to make the ceremony. The computer will also accompany the couple on their honeymoon, where she will be hitting "submit" while he tries to "enter." In a year, they'll both be running for the "esc" button.

MSNBC reported that the 1.5 million bats that hang out under a bridge in Austin—and are viewed by countless spectators every day—are going hungry as a result of the drought there. Not for nothin', but "bats" and "hungry" are two words you don't ever want to hear in the same sentence, no?

The Physicians Committee for Responsible Medicine says that hot dogs are as dangerous for you as cigarettes. Yeah, don't I know it? I've been on the cheeseburger patch for a week now . . . messy, but I haven't had a single hot dog.

Swedish officials enlisted volunteers to hand out lollipops to sots leaving the bars at closing time with the theory that the lollys will remove bad feelings from the minds of inebriates. I can't think of an easier way to get your ass kicked than to hand a drunk a lolly and say "Here, suck this" . . . in Swedish, no less.

A British man was caught on videotape stealing a two-hundred-dollar jacket. He was arrested at his home. When he arrived for his court date, you guessed it, he wore said jacket, security-tag rip holes and all.

An Ohio woman, who had recently given birth, got drunk at a wedding and began fighting with her husband. She was arrested after she sprayed the cops with breast milk. The police there are clearly lactose intolerant.

The BBC introduced a device called Wimbledon Net Mix, which enables users to lower the sound of the grunting and up the commentary volume. With some of those players, people had complained that they thought they were watching Showtime's *Real Sex* instead of the Women's finals.

A Russian woman was declared dead from a heart attack by doctors in the facility where she had been hospitalized. She was about to be buried when she woke up, saw her grieving relatives, realized she was at her own funeral, and quickly had a heart attack which killed her . . . for real. Yikes. Somewhere, Rod Serling is snickering and saying "Been there, done that."

Nogales, a town in Mexico that has been the home to enormous drug violence, holds a three-day tequila festival each year in order to boost tourism and restore confidence to the public that a visit there is not a "death sentence." Drug cartels, wasted underage teenagers, free tequila in a Mexican border town—yep, definitely high on the "things to do this weekend" charts. Gotta remember to bring the whole family.

An Ohio woman driving drunk was spotted by cops, led them through the drive-in window of a Taco Bell, and wouldn't pullover until she got her food. And what about the Florida guy who handed a bank teller a note to "fill up the bag" but forgot to bring the bag? People these days.

Alaska Airlines announced that they swapped out pilot manuals for iPads. I don't know about you, but I kind of want the pilot of an aircraft often weighing in excess of five hundred thousand pounds to have the how-to instructions COMMITTED TO MEMORY! Let's hope the batteries stay charged. "Hey, Bob before we get started, do *you* remember my password?"

TechNews Daily says that the Apple store in NYC is the most photographed attraction—more than the Statue of Liberty or the Empire State Building. I'm sure some think it's the unique design, but I'm betting it is so visitors can look at the photos wistfully later and remember where all their money went.

New research shows that adults who smoked marijuana before age fifteen may later have significant problems with attention span, impulse control, and other basic functions. How ridiculous. Do they mean that it could affect kmdkkl;;;; jsejjt nna and or may even affect your lakfpspp sjajj and tpppppppying?

The coffee industry announced that coffee prices keep going up. They'd best be careful . . . two more price raises and they'll be getting close to what Starbucks already charges.

In a bizarre accident, a New Zealand truck driver slipped and fell on a compressed air hose that pierced his buttocks and started to fill his body full of hot air. He survived and will now throw his hat into the next GOP presidential race.

In a survey called, "Sex and Secularism," a psychologist determined that atheists have the best sex lives, and that there is a direct correlation between guilt and sexual behavior. What wasn't clear was whose name was yelled out at the climactic moment?

News

The Japanese invented "mood ears," bunny-like ears worn on your head that are attached to a sensor on your forehead. They flop down when you're sad, point straight up when you concentrate, and wiggle when you're amused . . . yikes. Warning: Wear them when participating in other bunny activities and they can go so fast, you'll hover above your bed.

In recent years, people in Asian countries have been flocking to plastic surgeons in order to achieve a more "Western" look. McDonald's, Burger King, and Wendy's have all taken note and will be opening up three thousand new locations throughout the continent.

Researchers now say that hand sanitizer could possibly cause positive results in a urine drug test. How many times do we have to say this? You should *only* use it on your hands.

An Oregon woman was kicked off an Amtrak train for talking on the phone—for sixteen straight hours! Other than sleep, I can't think of *anything* I would want to do for that length of time. The weird part is the ride was only scheduled to be two hours long. It was Amtrak, after all.

A recent poll says that 61 percent of Americans are in favor of same-sex marriage. The other 39 percent may have not understood the question. One respondent said, "It's marriage . . . the same sex day in, day out . . . why would I be in favor of that?"

An exotic dancer from the US stunned British TV viewers when she appeared on a morning program showing off her breast implants, which weigh more than fifty pounds. She went to Britain because that operation is not allowed here in the states. Go figure. Her coolest dance move? Freefalling forward and bouncing right back up again.

An Oregon woman awoke from dental surgery with a British accent. Vocal changes after a procedure are unusual but not unique, as there have been cases of this reported in the past. For example, I usually talk in a falsetto after my prostate exam.

Saw an article about a Salt Lake City woman who was arrested after she asked an undercover officer to give her drugs in exchange for a salad. You've gotta admire her pluck, though. It can't be easy to find a drug dealer who's also in need of green, leafy vegetables.

News

The Icelandic Phallogical Museum finally got its first human specimen. Donated by his family, the penis of a deceased ninety-five-year old man will be joining a bevy of whale, seal, bear, and other mammal appendages. However, this one will be housed in the newly built Bobbitt wing of the museum.

A British company has brewed the first beer laced with Viagra. Called Royal Virility Performance, it was first brewed for the Royal Wedding. Drink it fast, though, or you'll get a stiff neck.

The state of Texas raised the speed limit to eighty-five miles per hour on some test roads. Quick math problem: If you start in Dallas and drive eighty-five miles per hour for ten hours, where are you? Answer: Still in the middle of nowhere.

In 2014, Florida considered the passing of a "baggy pants" bill that would fine anyone caught wearing them at their knees instead of up around the chest like most of the population there. With the Florida economy still spiraling downward and crime on the rise, it's good to see the legislature has their priorities straight. What's next? A "Minimum-Acceptable-Time-for-a-Left-Turn-Signal" bill?

Cops near Pittsburgh airport complained because prostitutes working nearby were accepting gift cards as payment. Cash was much easier to spot. Additionally, when they ask "How much?" the response of "fifty dollars plus shipping and handling fees" might screw with the entrapment laws.

Although USDA officials inspect everything coming out of Japan, sushi lovers are balking at eating the delicacies coming from the country and the sushi industry is worried. Damn, I was SO looking forward to having a three-headed Spider roll and finding a tapeworm in my salmon.

MOTW—an Ohio man was arrested for aggravated assault and obstruction after he barked and hissed at a dog sitting in a police car at the scene of an accident. Asked why, he responded, "The dog started it." Yeah, and it wasn't so much the dog's barking as the tone he took and the language he used. Yikes.

News

The President of the American College of Surgeons resigned after writing an editorial that stated "semen has a mood-enhancing effect on women." What a maroon. I think most women wish it were closer to Lifesavers and came in eight different flavors.

A mortuary in Compton, California, created the first "drive-thru" funeral parlor so motorists/mourners don't have to worry about parking. The body is on display in a window so you can use the drive-thru lane to sign the book, pay your respects, and then drive off. Why not just pair with Burger King and make it all one-stop shopping?

Astronomers located a brown dwarf star that is burning at a relatively low temperature of two hundred degrees. However, there was a heated discussion in the science community whether it is an actual "dwarf" star or a "mini-*me*-teor."

It's getting ridiculous. In 2013, Apple filed a lawsuit against Amazon for using the term "app store," claiming the copyright to those words. In a weird countersuit, Mother Nature also sued Apple for copyright infringement on the use of the name of one of her fruits. And word is there's a farmer out there talking to a lawyer about the word "Dell."

Two men were watching porn in separate booths at an Atlantic City adult bookstore when they heard a commotion and rushed out in time to stop a robbery that was taking place. The owner and the arresting officer were quite grateful and vigorously nodded their approval to both patrons, rather than shake hands.

Census takers in England are trying to prevent a repeat of the 2001 census where many people listed Warlock or Witch as their occupation and over four hundred thousand people listed "Jedi" as their religion. I thought I was bad for waiting to hear Elizabeth sing "Bohemian Rhapsody."

Hooters offered a doctor's note and a free appetizer to anyone who skipped work to come to their restaurants and watch the NCAA Tourney games. . . . Huh . . . gives a whole new meaning to the phrase "filling out the brackets."

News

A condom company came out with a line of condoms with advertisements printed right on the latex. Do they really think that someone, in the middle of slapping one of those puppies on, would stop and say, "Hey, I need to get my taxes done and H&R Block is just the place!" While others might say "Stop trying to put words in my mouth."

Students at Florida International University of Miami graduated wearing gowns made of recycled plastic bottles. The school is taking the "green" movement even further, printing diplomas on used toilet paper, offering a basic comment on what a degree is worth in today's economy.

A 2011 study published by the CDC journal *Emerging Infectious Diseases* says that sleeping with a pet can be quite unhealthy . . . especially if you don't write or call afterwards.

If you want a tomato on a Wendy's sandwich, you're going to have to ask for it. As produce prices rise, many fast food chains are trying to find ways to cut costs and this is Wendy's solution. Taco Bell will be doing something similar with beef.

Colorado passed a law that levies a 2.9 percent sales tax on bull semen. Plus a five cent deposit for the bottle. Prairie oysters remain tax-free.

An elderly Arizona man missed his exit and was stranded in the desert for five days after his car broke down. He said he survived by drinking windshield-wiper fluid. The reporter interviewing him couldn't get the whole story, as the man kept going back and forth, back and forth, back and forth. . . .

A woman in England adopted a rescued Jack Russell terrier but brought him back two days later. The reason? The color of his fur, ginger and white, clashed with her curtains. More irony: her first husband left her because the carpet didn't match the drapes.

An Italian couple was arrested for killing the woman's ex-husband by shoving a giant slab of butter down his throat. They thought he would choke (which he did) and that the butter would melt (which it didn't) and

News

that it would have been the perfect crime. The ironic part? He fell and hit his head on the floor which was . . . *parkay.*

A 2011 study discovered that the birds that inhabit the areas around Chernobyl have developed smaller brains than normal . . . which helps explain why people who live near Three Mile Island still root for the Steelers.

"Flowers wilt. Chocolate melts. Roaches are forever." That was a come-on in an ad from the Bronx Zoo. For ten dollars, you can give your special someone the ultimate V-Day gift by naming one of the thousands of Madagascar hissing roaches after them. Hand her/him that card and just watch their face for an unforgettable reaction.

Chocolate specialists are warning that that world's chocolate supply could soon dry up. When I told this to my wife, her eyes glazed over and she immediately began quoting scriptures: "In the beginning, the Lord created chocolate, and he saw that it was good. . . . Something needs to be done."

Researchers released a study that showed that the daily consumption of diet soda leads to a higher risk of stroke and heart attack. Yep, gotta be the diet Cokes. No way it's the bag of double bacon cheeseburgers.

A four-hundred-pound cow washed up on the beach in Seattle. Authorities were dumbfounded but local surfers mourned the death of the mystical surfing bovine. "Cow-abunga, dude."

A Columbia University sociology professor claimed that Facebook was the new place for hookers to sell sex. Before you plan to pick up one on your way home, know that this is complicated and done through a variety of code words and phrases. One such way involves going into Farmville and inquiring whether the back forty needs plowing. Or so I hear.

A seven-year-old boy mistakenly bought a fighter jet on eBay. It's embarrassing. I feel bad for the kid, I feel bad for the parents, but mostly, I feel really bad for the UPS delivery guy.

News

There's an iPhone app designed to help Catholics through confession. When you're done, just say three Hail Wozniaks and two Our Steve Jobs. You can also tithe 10 percent of your phone bill payment. Tweet me, Father, for I have sinned. What's the difference between God and Jobs? God never walked around thinking he was Steve Jobs or [Insert favorite megalomaniac name here].

A Marist College study reported that most Americans would choose the ability to read minds as their superpower. I think it would be eye-opening how many Buddha-like people would find their fellow humans filled with "emptiness" and "nothingness." And remember, eternal nothingness is fine if you happen to be dressed for it.

A sewage plant in Russia uses snails to monitor the levels of air pollution in the methane gas coming off the facility. Note to self: Never, ever order the Russian escargot.

Three men in Florida went on a spree robbing Babies R Us stores—for diapers. They were caught blocks away from their last job, trying to sell them at an apartment complex. They will soon be absorbed into the penal system and it's a sure bet they won't be pampered.

A recent bill passed in 2016 requires Toyota, among other hybrid car manufacturers, to make their models louder so blind people can hear them coming. They're Toyotas. . . . You'd think they would be able to hear the screams coming from inside the car, once the brakes or steering malfunctioned.

A Wisconsin postal carrier wanted to cheer up a woman on his route who seemed "stressed out." He told the woman he would deliver the mail to her office completely naked to make her laugh. The woman dared him to do it, so he brought the mail wearing only a smile. He was immediately arrested and jailed. She must not have wanted to sign for his package.

An Argentinean Archbishop told hundreds of kids that "there is no such thing as Santa," that he's a fantasy and they should stick to reality . . . and that presents come from Jesus. Huh.

News

In related news, a recent study says that most kids don't believe in Santa after the age of eight . . . and the ones that do, grow up to be Mets fans.

TSA agents in LAX formed a choir to serenade people standing in line, waiting to go through security. Most popular request? "Can you feel what I feel?"

Walmart considered installing wine-vending machines in their stores. Problem was that the machines never actually worked. How is that different from the rest of the shit I buy there? Had they worked they could have set them up right next to the gun department. "I'd like a good sweet red wine that goes with a thirty ought six."

Life is a WB cartoon. Sharks in Egypt killed and injured multiple tourists near a Red Sea resort. The problem was solved when a drunk did a cannonball off a diving board over the ocean and landed on the Mako's head, killing it instantly. The drunk was hospitalized for alcohol poisoning. Nothing to say. Next time, if it's a Great White, they're gonna need a bigger drunk.

Mackies of Scotland sells their award-winning Haggis-flavored potato chips on the web. The bulk of them are sold in Colorado. Given the proliferation of the marijuana businesses, it's a sure bet that people there will eat just about anything.

Crazy temperatures in the Arctic are resulting in new breeds of hybrid animals—grizzlies crossed with polar bears, belugas crossed with narwhals . . . But how cool would it be to see a caribou with the ability to shoot back? C'mon, everybody loves a fair fight.

The site of the world's worst nuclear disaster in history is now a tourist attraction. Yes, you can take a tour bus into Chernobyl's Exclusion Zone. Once inside, you are warned not to touch anything or even sit on the ground. When you leave, body scanners test for high levels of radiation. If the alarm sounds, the guards will wash off any radioactive dust before you're allowed on the bus. Visitors return rested and aglow.

A Canadian atheist group unveiled an ad campaign at bus stops and the like, extolling the virtues of atheism and claiming that the traditional deities are as much a figment of the collective imagination as UFOs are. You know what you get when you cross an atheist with a Jehovah's Witness? Someone who rings your doorbell for no reason.

A city in Germany levied a "pleasure tax," forcing prostitutes to purchase tickets for days they work. Hopefully, they won't require the same for their customers. It'd be like being at Disney World—two hours waiting in line for a five-minute ride.

In Germany, Police arrested a man who decorated a six-foot pot plant as if it were a Christmas tree. Did he also do a Nativity scene in pipes and bongs? Germany is evidently becoming Pot Central. Munich police detained a twenty-one-year-old man after he had created a homemade advent calendar that, instead of chocolates, had cannabis behind each door. I'm sure all the candy was eaten by day three. 'Tis the season.

A British woman was so hooked on Twitter, she sent out over a hundred tweets while she was in labor and giving birth. Of course, most of the tweets looked like this: "Motherf#$%&ing, C#$%ksu$#%er, Get it out!

Get it out, you f#$%$ing a%$$ole!!!!!! OMG, OMG ... TTFN."

ABC News reported that there has been an upswing in teens snorting nutmeg—a cheap high and, in large enough doses, a serious hallucinogenic. Word of caution: Snort *before* you put it on the eggnog.

Wayne State University pulled the Helen Thomas Spirit of Diversity Award because of the anti-Semitic remarks she made. In other news, the Klan has established a scholarship in her honor at the Vienna School of Fine Arts.

Singapore rebuked its national water polo team for wearing swim trunks that feature an "inappropriate" likeness of the city-state's flag. The suits were designed by the team itself. Maybe they were just tired of telling their girlfriends, "Baby, it's the pool, it's not you."

A poll conducted on Petfinder.com says that 63 percent of pet dogs receive Christmas presents while only 58 percent of cat owners buy for their furry felines. Seems reasonable: dogs make a list; cats just can't be bothered.

News

By observing the breeding habits of the white ibis, a scientific study group concluded that mercury pollution is resulting in males of the species mating with each other. So now the only place you'll be able to see them is on Fire Island . . . and what about the swallow?

A bank robber in the Boston area, dubbed the "U30 Bandit" for his ability to get in and out in well under thirty seconds, was caught and sentenced to twenty-five years. Asked for her thoughts on how upset she is, his girlfriend said, "Not so much. Between you and me, he was also the 'U30 Lover.'"

Charles Manson was caught with a cell phone hidden in the mattress in his prison cell. He was evidently calling and texting people around the country. Man, would you answer that text? Just imagine the number of voices in his head now. He must need a family plan.

A Wisconsin woman was arrested for biting off her husband's tongue when he tried to kiss her. She is now undergoing psychological evaluation. Could have been worse . . . could have been his brisket.

A company called Kine2b, a medicinal pot collective, offers a delivery service in the San Francisco area. Hopefully they're following the Domino's model and offering two free joints if it takes longer than thirty minutes. I'm sure everyone would benefit. Come to think of it, they could make a fortune pairing up with one of the fast food companies, no? One-stop pot shopping . . .

Bloomberg Daily reports that American teens in the US ranked thirty-first out of thirty-five countries in math. One participant exclaimed, "Well, at least we're in the top 50 percent!"

Patrons at a pub in Devon, England, were not amused when a tractor carrying ten tons of manure crashed into the building, dumping all its cargo over the entire bar and all over everyone/everything inside. Gives new meaning to the phrase "getting shit-faced," eh?

The FAA did not pursue action against an NJ pilot who tossed rolls of toilet paper from a small plane onto an athletic field as a test run for a streamer drop at an upcoming high school football game. He circled the school athletic fields in his Cessna 172 and dropped two rolls of toilet paper. People called the police and he was arrested, but his record was wiped clean.

In a WebMD survey of ten thousand doctors, some 12 percent said it would be okay to become romantically or sexually involved with a patient if they waited at least six months after treatment. "Hey, since that rash went away, wanna have dinner?"

A government study says nearly one in five Americans—45.9 million people—suffered from some form of mental illness. While incredibly disconcerting, it does explain quite a bit.

The Pope changed his position on contraception and approved the use of condoms in special cases . . . like to reduce the risk of infection, or for filling them up with water and dropping them off buildings. (That's why St. Peter's Square always looks wet. Those crazy Cardinals.) Way to get with the times, *fahder.*

An Upstate NY middle school principal, not believing it when a mother called her two sons in sick, drove to their house, walked in, went to their room, and tried to force them out of their sick bed and go to school. He has since been suspended. He's lucky he didn't get shot. Bueller? Bueller? Bueller?

A transgender golfer sued the LPGA so they would allow her to become a member. (Rimshot, please.) She was denied play in the Long Drivers championship, a competition she won in 2008, before they changed the rules to reflect the LPGA's. Irony on a base level? The event was sponsored by Dick's Sporting Goods.

Two pilots filed a lawsuit against the TSA ("We handle more packages than UPS") over having to be subjected to full-body scans and pat-downs. One said, "Hell, I'm a weapon. If I wanted to kill people, I could just crash the plane." And there goes the confidence levels of millions of passengers. Way to go, Sky King.

A nudist colony in Florida wanted to kick one of their tenants out because he doesn't live *au naturel* all the time. The homeowner's association says that's against the rules and he must go. Another patron said the man will be missed: "We have breakfast every morning and

he always carries two cups of coffee and a dozen doughnuts. . . . He's also very popular with the ladies."

Texas A&M had a "Code Maroon" security lockdown
when there were reports of a gunman present during a
visit by George Bush Sr. and Mrs. Bush. No gunman
was found, but Bugs Bunny is being sought for ques-
tioning.

The pastor of a New Jersey church wants his parishio-
ners to delete Facebook from their computers, claiming it inspires cheating and can lead to virtual adultery
(and he should know all about that . . .) Does he also
think Farmville leads to virtual bestiality? What a
maroon.

Police in India arrested a man at Chennai Airport
with over two thousand gems in his gut. No word on
what detection methods they used. Those wacky Sri
Lankans, they just think they shit diamonds, don't
they?

Some people are just bad at their job. An Indonesian
Shaman, who was sitting next to a volcano to make

sure the gods were appeased and it didn't erupt, was killed when . . . you guessed it . . . the volcano erupted and he was covered in lava. He had been told he had to stay there under any circumstances. Moral: please don't leave the Shaman.

NASA is contemplating a space mission to send astronauts to colonize Mars. The only problem? They will never return. Not such a problem . . . I have a complete list of volunteers. To name but a few: Charlie Sheen, Lindsay Lohan, Paris Hilton, Randy Quaid. Welcome to the Planet of the Misfit Toys.

A man who stole one thousand pieces of luggage from the Phoenix Airport was captured by the police. The cops proceeded with caution because they knew he'd be packing. He's being held at the Phoenix Zoo, where a giant gorilla keeps throwing him around its cage.

Remember 3D televisions? They were supposed to revolutionize the TV industry. Not surprisingly, sales of 3D television sets have been disappointing. Hey, Einstein, have you ever given any thought to maybe it's not the hardware? Maybe people will start buying more TVs when you start writing better shows. It's that simple. They haven't invented glasses yet that can make "moronic" into "smart."

Discovery News reported that pessimistic dogs see the bowl half empty. Just out of curiosity, how does one determine if a dog is optimistic or pessimistic? "No way is he gonna pet me . . . No way . . . And, if he does, he won't mean it . . . Yeah, the bowl is down but put more food in there? Not a chance . . . I'd bet money on it . . . Like he'd even take me for a walk, the lazy bastard . . . Not gonna happen. You watch."

Chilean miners revealed after being rescued that there was a point where they joked about cannibalism. Thankfully, they stayed calm and didn't get into a stew about it.

Three economists won the Nobel Prize for a job market theory that discusses why people remain unemployed when there are jobs available. The paper also postulates that the current economy can turn around quickly. Apparently, they won the prize for Fiction.

A woman that was working at a newly-opened funeral parlor staved off a thief looking for cash when she began throwing cremations urns at him until he ran off. There wasn't a lot of money to be had but, you know, a penny saved . . .

A set of English conjoined twins made the news when they moved from London to a small town in Ohio. When asked why they moved to the US, it was explained that the other brother wanted to drive for a while.

A Chicago woman, who was a huge White Sox fan, sued a tattoo artist for inking dyslexia. She had wanted "SOX" on her leg but ended up with "XOS." Now everywhere she goes, people blow kisses and give her hugs. Go figure.

Police in New York arrested eight longshoremen and others in a sting that uncovered nearly one ton of cocaine being smuggled in from Panama, valued at thirty-four million. A ton . . . that's so much that even Tony Montana would say: "No, I'm good."

News

A man in Arizona survived an attack by his roommates. The reason? He refused to let them suck his blood. Evidently, both of them are "vampires" and had done it before. This particular day, he came home from a local Red Cross Blood Drive and was a pint short. He said, "No dear, not tonight, I have a headache" and they went bat shit crazy. The man said later, "That's it, I've had it. They're undead to me."

According to tests given in England, kids there believe that Buzz Lightyear was the first man on the moon and that the Star Wars *Death Star* is the furthest planet from the sun. They also think Darwin invented the telephone. To their credit, though, most kids answered "false" when asked if a person could survive an anvil falling on them from atop a high cliff or if cars are powered by feet.

An Ohio woman invented a new game. It's called "Imbecile." Here's how you play: Go up to a random police officer, give him your name, and ask if there are any outstanding warrants on you. If there are, run like hell. If you get caught, go to jail. If not, play again. Fun, huh? One thing: There are no extra points for getting tased.

A park in Massachusetts experimented with lighting that runs on energy generated from dog poop. Owners scoop up their pet's droppings and deposit them into a biodegradable bag, which is deposited into a tank that produces methane gas that lights up the lights. And not very well, I might add. More than one person walking on the lit pathways has said "I can't see shit."

Prosecutors in Washington State arrested a woman who plunged a steak knife into a man's back because he made fun of the smell of her feet. The trouble started when she was drinking and hanging out with friends and was challenged to do a back flip. When she took off her shoes to do it, the teasing started. Good thing they didn't ask her to do a split. He'd be dead.

A woman in China sued a theater chain for "subjecting" her to twenty minutes of ads before the movie she was seeing started. Hey, why don't you do what they do here? Come in twenty-five minutes after the announced start time, sit directly in front of me, and continue talking on your cell phone. And slurping . . . lots of slurping . . . even without a drink.

News

A scientific study claims that elevator buttons are dirtier than toilet seats. Apparently, a typical button harbors nearly forty times as many germs as a public toilet seat. I get that, and I'm all for public safety, but don't they realize how hard it is to push the floor you want with your ass? It's almost impossible to get it on the first try.

A Montana woman fought off a bear that was attacking one of her dogs using a zucchini. The bear took a swipe at her and she threw the zucchini, scaring him off. You know, if I was sitting down about to enjoy a juicy steak dinner and someone threw a salad at me, I'd run away, too.

Two American tourists were arrested and charged with "desecrating the dead" when Greek customs agents found six human skulls in their luggage. They claimed they were fakes and that they'd bought them in a gift shop on Mykonos. Let that be a lesson to all the travelers out there: getting head in a foreign country is always risky business.

A visitor to a Wild West-themed museum in Dodge City, Kansas, nearly hung himself by placing his head in a display noose. "Now, son, never, ever, do this or else you might . . . aaaaaaccckkk." Taking stupidity to new heights.

Scientists at Boeing are developing a plane that that could fly for five years without landing to which officials at LaGuardia, O'Hare, and Detroit Airport replied, "Been there, done that."

Evidently a big controversy emerged when a number of students in New Zealand were videotaped throwing possum carcasses around. Of course, it went viral. (How could you not see that coming?) The idiot principal explained that it "teaches them about nature." Yeah, right. Let's make it a fair fight and try tossing them while they're still alive. Having one of those suckers clamp down on your jugular will most definitely teach you all you need to know about nature.

The Cooper's Hill cheese-rolling event went off without a hitch this year, even in spite of police trying to stop it multiple times in recent years. The cause of countless injuries in the past, the two-hundred-year-old event consists of chasing a giant roll of local fromage down a very steep hill. Ah yes, the Brits and their cheese. Have a gouda time.

The Vatican's prosecutor of clerical sex abusers stated that they will suffer "eternal damnation in Hell" for their crimes. Yeah . . . maybe . . . but we can find something a little closer to home . . . like, I dunno, castration? If you want to stay with the biblical thing, I hear a thousand locusts in your pants works wonders, too.

A man who swallowed an abundance of erectile dysfunction pills was admitted to the hospital after he remained hard for twenty-seven hours. When doctors told him they would have to amputate, he fled to the Dominican Republic, where he got a job as a stripper pole in a gentleman's club.

An inmate at a Washington prison, out on a work furlough, smuggled the following—a cigarette lighter, rolling papers, a golf-ball sized baggie of tobacco, the same amount of pot, a small pipe, a bottle of tattoo ink, and eight needles—in, you guessed it, his *rectum* (damn near killed him). He was eventually caught and thrown into solitary. His new jailhouse name is now "Clown Car."

Moron of the week: A guy dials 911 instead of 119, trying to reach his drug dealer in a local hotel. The police respond and both are arrested for possession of heroin. The caller was next door, in room 118. I guess smack takes away the ability to just bang on the wall.

I love it when big oil companies refer to an oil "spill"? I think not. "Spill" is something your child does with his milk. "Spill" is something your Aunt takes that your mother gets upset about, i. e. "Your Aunt Judy took a nasty spill." What we usually have (aside from a failure to communicate) is an oil GUSH. Twenty-three million gallons . . . or roughly what is needed to fill half of the SUVs in New Jersey.

A study was published that said older women should watch the scale, as weight gain can lead to the slowing of mental acuity. How about with men? These days, if

News

I can get the label of my shirt *behind* me and on the inside, I'm having a cocktail.

A man arrested for brutally kicking and blinding his girlfriend's dog was released with two hundred hours of community service at a local animal shelter. Doesn't seem fair. How about we wrap him in duct tape and use him for pit bull training? His girlfriend said "He's sorry, but it's just a dog and society needs to get its priorities straight."

A school in Montana considered teaching extensive sex education to kindergarteners. Included in the curriculum would be gay sex, kink, and a complete look at all the various sexual positions. And to think, up to now all they had to worry about was the kids eating the crayons.

A mother found an S&M mag in her ten-year-old's closet. Upset, she asked her husband what he thinks they should do. "Well, I definitely wouldn't spank him."

New slogan for Apple: "We're not Microsoft, but we might just be Hasbro."

A New Hampshire couple said their twenty-five-pound pet tortoise reappeared almost four years after escaping from its pen. Asked where he'd gone, he replied: "About one hundred yards."

Cops in Dublin found a penguin that had been kidnapped from the city zoo and brought to the northern part of town. No motive as to why, but if you factor in too many pints of Guinness, maybe these idiots thought they were snatching a nun?

A truck driver was stopped for reckless endangerment after his eighteen-wheeler was seen swerving all over the road. Why? He was trying to do dental surgery on himself. He had tied one end of a string to the aching tooth and the other to the top of the cabin and was waiting for "a big bump." *The Three Stooges* meets *BJ and the Bear.*

A truck carrying thirty-nine thousand pounds of shredded cheese caught fire on the highway and blocked traffic for hours. It took firefighter six hours to put it out, primarily because they had to fight off hundreds of people trying to get close with little pieces of bread on forks.

BP Gas considered changing the name of their stations to something with a more PR-friendly connotation. Being considered: Mussolini Motoring, Pol Pot Petrol, and Genocide Gas.

An Ohio woman claimed she was surfing Facebook where she discovered her husband was married to a second wife. She found a complete album of pictures from his "other wedding." Ya know, this "friending" thing has gotten way out of hand; now she needs to find a lawyer who specializes in "unfriending."

The current CEO of BP, Bob Dudley, continued the tradition of idiotic statements set by his predecessor. He was actually quoted as saying "it's time to begin scaling back parts of the oil spill cleanup." I'm thinking they must send these guys to "I-Hate-Public-Relations" school or something.

LA Firefighters responded to a blaze at an empty house in Grenada Hills and discovered a huge pot-growing operation in the garage. They put out the fire and called the police—from a Pizza Hut down the street, nearly two days later.

A cell phone store manager in Florida deterred an armed man from robbing the store by telling him "Jesus wouldn't approve." The man pulled a gun on her and said he attended church and wasn't a bad person. She repeated "Jesus wouldn't approve, Jesus wouldn't approve." Finally, Jesus Gonsalves, the assistant manager, came out of the back room with a shotgun and it was over. They both can't wait to testify.

A drug dealer in California was arrested for selling cocaine *and* for keeping his dead girlfriend in his upscale hotel room . . . for a year. Apparently, after she overdosed, he put her in a plastic box and covered her in dry ice. The dealer wasn't available for comment but the room service manager stated: "We should have known. Every day: turkey club, pot of coffee, two hundred pounds of dry ice. Every day." Ah, the things we do for love.

A fan, sitting in the front row at Yankee Stadium, was hit in the face by a fair ball while talking on his cell phone. Good. Here's an idea, Sparky: watch the game. (Not to mention the tickets probably cost as much as that phone.) Schmuck.

A study says that 80 percent of women fake orgasms during sex. Many say they do it because of time limitations. Why is there a line? Maybe there should be a twenty-four second clock, like in the NBA? Or a speed clock like in chess?

Public Service Warning: Nearly twenty thousand people are sent to the emergency room every year over Fourth of July weekend. Be safe—when you grill, wear a condom.

The Internet Corporation for Assigned Names and Numbers (ICANN) started the process to approve .xxx as the domain name for pornography. Does that mean that the next time my mother sends "hugs" at the end of her email she'll pull up *Hooker Cheerleaders 3?*

Tourism officials in New Orleans took some flak for an ad that stated "This isn't the first time New Orleans survived the British." Some folks thought it too xenophobic. Hey, they're really gonna hate the ad campaign from Florida: "We haven't seen this much oil since Don Johnson's hair."

According to *Forbes* magazine, an MIT student won the 2012 Move an Asteroid Technical Paper Competition by postulating a theory that if an earth-killing asteroid were headed toward us, it could be stopped by using paintballs. Not sure about the techie jargon, but evidently most asteroids are sore losers and if hit, they'd take their paintball guns and find another galaxy.

A California-based energy drink company disputed the exceedingly high caffeine content rating on their product that was issued by Consumer Reports. The Sambazon Company's PR department issued a 1,100-page response, just about eleven minutes after they initially received the damaging report.

A new poll says that Americans are beginning to feel better about the economy and have begun to accept the new normal, having long since passed through the other stages—denial, anger, bargaining, and depression.

News

An intoxicated Pittsburgh man mistakenly shot a costumed nine-year old girl at a Halloween party, thinking she was a skunk . . . huh . . . a skunk the size of a nine-year-old? Jeez, that would give off a stink they could smell in New Jersey.

A wealthy Wall Street stockbroker donated one hundred million to Central Park to be used to maintain the foliage. Okay, ready? Here it comes . . . He's a HEDGE FUND MANAGER! (Hey, you've been a beautiful audience . . . Try the veal . . . Goodnight!)

Toyota made a Prius hearse. So be prepared for funeral processions weaving in and out of traffic at ridiculous speeds while pretending to be good for the environment.

Travel & Leisure magazine ran a survey that places New York City on top for dirtiest, loudest, and rudest city in the country. Tell us something we didn't know. "G'head, ya asshole, ask me sumthin' stoopid again, ya friggin' imbecile," said pretty much everyone from New York who answered the questionnaire.

The pilots of an American Eagle flight leaving JFK had to return to the gate for a new crew after two stewardesses got into a heated fight. Hey, American Airlines, instead of landing, turn a negative into a positive; open up all those Jell-O cups, throw 'em in the aisle, and give the passengers something to watch instead of those *Big Bang Theory* reruns.

A Dr. Pepper ad that ran on Facebook sparked a minor controversy. In a variation of the famous March of Progress illustration, its first image is an ape-like creature on all fours, which is described as "Pre-Pepper." Then, an early-evolution man, standing erect, finds a can of Dr. Pepper. Finally, a true human, drinking Dr. Pepper is identified as "Post-Pepper." Of course, many creationists weighed in and railed against the use of these images. "I ain't no freakin' chimp!" one ex-fan of the soft drink screamed . . . then flung feces at his computer and went back to masturbating.

BPI (Beef Products Inc.) filed a billion-dollar suit against ABC and three reporters for doing a piece on "Pink Slime," the filler food product made of connective tissue, beef scraps, and chemicals. They maintained

News

the piece was slanderous and did "irreparable" damage. Hey fellas, methinks your problems began when you started calling the stuff "pink slime."

Talk about irony. Two TSA screeners kicked a woman off a flight for having a bad attitude. Let's see: ridiculous lines, long waits, shoe removal, verbal abuse, scanning, full-body cavity searches, minimal food, overcrowding, delays, all kinds of abuse . . . Guess these dropkicks found it hard to believe she wouldn't be in a state of pure ecstasy.

File this under: No Shit? The latest trend amongst the world's vapid is . . . anal tattoos.

Sacrebleu! Due to worries about their own image, the French government put up antirudeness billboards around Paris and "good manners" seminars were conducted throughout the country. *Le Monde* interviewed several people on the streets and found that most Parisians answered "I fart in your general direction" and "Your mother was a hamster and your father smelt of elderberries."

An Oklahoma City woman was arrested after she attacked her boyfriend with a power drill during a domestic dispute. She defended her actions by saying that she's intensely literal and was only reacting to his constant pleas to screw him.

Chinese athletes are repeatedly accused of using performance-enhancing drugs during the Olympics. It's shameful. The good news is that the NFL has set up a recruiting office in their hotel lobby.

The US Postal Service defaulted on a $5.7 billion payment. (And I get a call when my credit cards are a week late.) It didn't stop the mail; it just pushed delivery back a little more. Last week, I got my 2007 Nordstrom Holiday catalog.

India's huge power outage in 2012 cut power for six hundred million people. Again, six hundred million people. Tech support from the States suggested they unplug the generators, count to fifteen, and plug them in again to see if that helps.

News

A California man was arrested at LAX trying to smuggle four pounds of meth inside Snickers bars. Jeez, that stuff is highly addictive . . . and meth is bad news, too.

Conclusion

"Sarcasm I now see to be, in general, the language of the devil; for which reason I have long since as good as renounced it."
—Thomas Carlyle

Well, that's it.

Please exit the car from the right and don't forget to take all your belongings.

For all of you who totally enjoyed the ride and are left in a postorgasmic afterglow, didn't you learn anything? What were you doing back there? Now go back, reread it, and I want to see you come back with some serious 'tude.

For the rest of you, yeah, right back at you.

Okay, is everyone back now?

Don't want any of you to feel bad, so you know what? Let's make believe this is your kid's middle school soccer team.

That's right, EVERYBODY is a winner. Trophies all around.

We'll wait to put on our big kid pants at the end of the next book. *(S)